AF531606

Preface

Thermodynamics and Heat Engine aims to serve as a text book for undergraduate graduate and postgraduate students of engineering and physics branches. The book covers various examples and illustrations as per the syllabus prescribed by the UP Technical University covering the entire curriculum.

Thermodynamics and Heat Engine enables the students to know and understand the relation which exists among physics and other related subjects which becomes difficult to understand among students. Due to its extra knowledge and easy explanations the book is quiet reputed among the engineers and industrialists.

Author

Chapter 1

Thermodynamics

THERMODYNAMICS PROPERTIES

INTRODUCTION

This chapter covers notes on certain important thermodynamic properties including enthalpy (h), Specific heat (c_v,c_p), gas constant (R), and Entropy (S)

ENTHALPY

In many thermodynamic fluid process analyses the sum of the internal energy (U) and the product of pressure (P) and volume(V) is present. The combination (U + PV) is called the enthalpy of the fluid.

H is a thermodynamic fluid property but is does not have an absolute value(because it includes internal energy U)value and therefore enthalpy changes are generally applied or enthalpy values are identified relative to a fixed state e.g. water at 273 deg.K. It is important to note that enthalpy is simply a combination of properties..it is not a form of stored energy although for certain applications it can be treated as energy.

$H = U + PV$..........(extensive property)

per unit mass

$h = u + Pv$...........(intensive property)

When referring for water and steam and other fluids at different states in tables the following enthalpy designations are used

- h_g..specific enthalpy of saturated vapour

- h_f..specific enthalpy of saturated liquid
- h_i..specific enthalpy of saturated solid
- h_{fg}..specific latent heat of vapourisation = $h_g - h_f$
- h_{if}..specific latent heat of fusion = $h_f - h_i$
- h_{ig}..specific heat of sublimation = $h_g - h_i$

SPECIFIC HEAT CAPACITY

The heat capacity of a substance is classically defined as the amount of heat needed to raise unit mass of a substance one degree Centigrade.

In SI units the specific heat capacity is the amount of heat required to raise 1 kg mass through 1 degree kelvin. (Unit kJ/kg.K). The specific heat of a substance is the ratio of the heat capacity of a substance relative to a reference substance generally water.

The heat capacity of water is one calorie per degree C (classical) or (4180 J/kg.K) The specific heat of a substance relative to water will be numerically equal to its heat capacity in classical units, but not in SI units

The term specific heat is often used when the heat capacity actually is meant. Because the heat capacities of most substances vary with changes in temperature, the temperatures of both the specified substance and the reference substance must be known in order to give a precise value for the specific heat.

SPECIFIC HEAT CAPACITIES OF GASES

Four specific heats are for gases are used.

- C_v = Molar specific heat at constant volume.
- C_p = Molar specific heat at constant pressure.
- c_v = Specific heat at constant volume.
- c_p = Specific heat at constant pressure.

The molar specific heats are mainly used for chemical studies. The specific heat varies with temperature and pressure.

The graph below this illustrates this characteristic for c_p. for air Table below show the variation of c_p and c_p with temperatures.

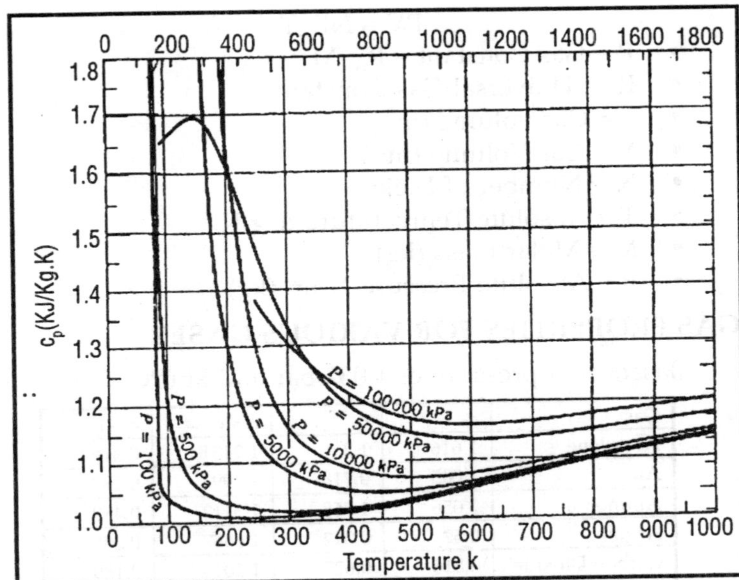

Fig. Variation of c_p (for Air) with temperature and pressure

Variation of cp (for Air) with temperature and pressure

LATENT HEAT

The latent heat of fusion is the amount of heat required to convert unit mass a substance from solid to liquid without change of temperature..

The latent heat of vapourisation is the amount of heat required to convert unit mass of a substance from liquid to vapour without change of temperature.

GAS CONSTANT R

The gas constant R is derived from the equation of state Pv = RT.. for unit mass of gas

$$PV = mRT$$

The gas constant R is different for each gas and has different units depending on the unit systems used. Typical units are (kJ/kg.K).

The universal gas constant R_u is the same for all gases and is defined by

$$PV = NR_uT$$

- R = Gas Constant = R_u /M
- R_u = Universal Gas Constant
- v = Gas volume (m^3)
- V = Gas Volume (m^3)
- N = Number of Moles
- T = Absolute Temperature deg K
- M = Molar mass (kg)
- P = Absolute Pressure N/m^3 (kg)

GAS PROPERTIES FOR VARIOUS GASES

Based on a pressure of 1.032 bar and at 0°C

Gas	c_p	c_v	c_p / c_v	c_p - c_v
Acetylene	1.616	1.3	1.2431	0.316
Air	1.005	0.718	1.3997	0.287
Ammonia	2.056	1.568	1.3112	0.488
Argon	0.52	0.312	1.6667	0.208
Carbon Dioxide	0.816	0.627	1.3014	0.189
Carbon Disulphide	0.582	0.473	1.2304	0.109
Carbon Monoxide	1.038	0.741	1.4008	0.297
Chlorine	0.473	0.36	1.3139	0.113
Coal Gas	2.14	1.59	1.3459	0.55
Ethylene	1.47	1.173	1.2532	0.297
Helium	5.2	3.121	1.6661	2.079
Hydrochloric Acid	0.795	0.567	1.4021	0.228
Hydrogen	14.05	9.934	1.4143	4.116
Hydrogen Sulphide	0.992	0.748	1.3262	0.244
Krypron	0.25	0.151	1.6556	0.099
Methane	2.19	1.672	1.3098	0.518
Neon	1.03	0.618	1.6667	0.412
Nitrogen	1.038	0.741	1.4008	0.297
Oxygen	0.909	0.649	1.4006	0.26
Propane	1.549	1.36	1.1390	0.189
Sulphur Dioxide	0.586	0.456	1.2851	0.13
Water Vapor	1.842	1.381	1.3338	0.461
Xenon	0.16	0.097	1.6495	0.063

THERMODYNAMIC PROPERTIES OF PLATINUM DIATOMICS

Thermodynamic properties of diatomic transition metal compounds are very important for investigating their thermal behaviour. Recently, these properties have been applied in the fabrication of smart devices using intelligent materials for examples using platinum).

Transition metal compounds have a wide range of actual and potential applications in materials science because of their relatively high melting points, moderate densities, and resistance to chemical attack.

Platinum-containing compounds have been used in nanoscience and nanotechnology. For example, alloys such as iron-platinum (FePt), are used as nanodots. Platinum itself is used in a wide range of applications, including catalytic converters for cars, fuel cell electrocatalysts, computer technology, optical communication, missile technology, neurosurgery and medical science.

The unique properties of platinum generate a high level of interest among scientists. Due to the presence of unpaired *d*electrons, which have a greater angular momentum than *s* and *p* electrons, more energy is needed for the excitation of Pt in the molecular phase. This requires a high energy excitation device such as a gas discharge laser, which leads to experimental difficulties. Thus the experimental study of platinum diatomics is very challenging and expensive.

Scientific groups such as the Scientific Group Thermodata Europe (SGTE), the Joint Institute of High Temperatures, Russian Academy of Sciences (IVTAN) and, in the U.S.A., the Joint Army-Navy-Air Force (JANAF) Thermochemical Working Group (6) and the National Aeronautics and Space Administration (NASA), are engaged in the critical assessment and compilation of thermodynamic data for different molecular species.

An early contribution to the development of thermodynamic properties was made by Tolman, for diatomic hydrogen. The credit for further development of the subject goes to Hicks and Mitchell, for their work on hydrogen chloride. Giauque and Overstreet implemented the technique suggested by Hicks and Mitchell for the calculation of these properties for hydrogen, chlorine and hydrogen chloride.

They modified the reported theory by using stretching and interaction terms for diatomic molecules. Gordon and Barnes calculated the thermodynamic properties of chlorine (Cl_2), bromine (Br_2), hydrogen chloride (HCl), carbon monoxide (CO), oxygen (O_2) and nitric oxide (NO) molecules. The study of thermodynamic properties of the phosphorous mononitride (PN) molecule was performed by McCallum and Liefer.

The thermodynamic properties of transition metal alloys were reported by Darby.Calculation of the partition function and thermodynamic properties of the rare gas atoms argon, krypton and xenon was performed by Elyutin *et al.* In the domain of theory of thermodynamic properties, Eu reported Boltzmann entropy, relative entropy and their related values. Chandra and Sharma calculated the partition function for carbon monosulfide (CS) and silicon monoxide (SiO) molecules. Recently Uttam and coworkers estimated the thermodynamic properties of potassium monohalides and alkaline earth metal monohydrides using partition function theory.

The data on thermodynamic properties have been reported for a large number of molecules but a survey of the literature reveals that the values of thermodynamic properties for some diatomic molecules are not yet reported accurately. Therefore we have estimated the thermodynamic properties of platinum monohydride (PtH), platinum monocarbide (PtC), platinum mononitride (PtN) and platinum monoxide (PtO) molecules using spectroscopic data and partition function theory. The choice of the temperature range from 100 K to 3000 K is due to the fact that this range of temperatures covers the applications of platinum from biological sciences to high-temperature chemistry and astrophysics. In the present paper, we report the values of thermodynamic properties Gibbs energy (*G*), enthalpy (*H*), entropy (*S*) and specific heat capacity at constant pressure (C_P) for PtH, PtC, PtN and PtO

RESEARCH METHODOLOGY IN ENGLISH

RESEARCH METHODOLOGY IN ENGLISH

Edited by
Sunita Chitrangad

OMEGA PUBLICATIONS
NEW DELHI - 110 002 (INDIA)

OMEGA PUBLICATIONS
4378/4B, G4, JMD House, Murari Lal Street,
Ansari Road, Daryaganj, New Delhi-110 002
Phone: 23278062, 65901906,
e-mail: omega_publications@yahoo.com

Research Methodology in English

First Published, 2017

ISBN 978-81-8455-101-3

PRINTED IN INDIA

Published by Mahendra Garg for Omega Publications, New Delhi - 110 002 and Printed at Tarun Offset Press, Delhi-110 053

Preface

For a researcher in English (both language and literature), first it is necessary to understand what English Studies is?

Generally, research in language and literature is conducted in most conventional way throughout the world. Being global lingua fanca, English is most sought after field of study which is evident from current choice of students being admitted to different universities for higher education.

So far research methodology is concerned, traditionally a set pattern is there. Major steps in this direction could be:

- Choose a topic: After a thorough study of research already/being conducted, the scholar is advised by the mentor to select a particular topic.
- Devising/Developing the synopsis.
- Search/Acquisition of all relevant literature from various sources.
- Extraction of essential material and it arrangement.
- Writing of the thesis.
- Evaluation and finalisation.

Amidst plenty of literature available, this book is unique which introduces you to the research domain of English in broad perspective. This will help you in finalising you research plan.

The main topics included herein are—Introduction; English Language: Origin and Development; English Literature; Indian English Literature; Research in Bilingual Proficiency Development; Various Linguistic Issues; Issues in English Phonetics; Theories of Communicative Competence; Glossary etc.

Substantially based on authentic sources, this book will prove a vade mécum to one and all concerned. I express my gratitude to various scholars, academics of repute, colleagues and friends for subscribing their views, guidance, and assistance. I am thankful to my publisher for undertaking this publication.

—**Editor**

Contents

1

Introduction

English studies is an academic discipline that includes the study of literatures written in the English language (including literatures from the U.K., U.S., Ireland, Canada, Australia, New Zealand, Hong Kong, the Philippines, India, South Africa, and the Middle East, among other areas), English linguistics (including English phonetics, phonology, syntax, morphology, semantics, pragmatics, corpus linguistics, and stylistics), and English sociolinguistics (including discourse analysis of written and spoken texts in the English language, the history of the English language, English language learning and teaching, and the study of World Englishes).

More broadly, English studies explores the production and analysis of texts produced in English (or in areas of the world in which English is a common mode of communication). It is not uncommon for academic departments of "English" or "English Studies" to include scholars of the English language, literature (including literary criticism and literary theory), linguistics, law, journalism, composition studies, the philosophy of language, literacy, publishing/history of the book, communication studies, technical communication, folklore, cultural studies, creative writing, critical theory, disability studies, area studies (especially American studies), theatre, gender studies/ethnic studies, digital media/electronic publishing, film studies/media studies, rhetoric and philology/etymology, and various courses in the liberal arts and humanities, among others.

In most English-speaking countries, the literary and cultural dimensions of English studies are typically practiced in university departments of English, while the study of texts produced in non-English languages takes place in other departments, such as departments of foreign language or comparative literature. English linguistics is often studied in separate departments of linguistics. This disciplinary divide between a dominant linguistic or a literary orientation is one motivation for the division of the North American Modern Language Association (MLA) into two subgroups. At universities in non-English-speaking countries, the same department often covers all aspects of English studies including linguistics: this is reflected, for example, in the structure and activities of the European Society for the Study of English (ESSE).

English Studies

Literature and linguistics, along with List of academic disciplines

- English linguistics
- English sociolinguistics
- Discourse analysis in English
- English stylistics (linguistics)
- World Englishes
- History of the English Language
- Composition studies

- Rhetoric
- Technical communication
- English language learning and teaching
- English Literature
  - American literature, including:
    - African American literature
    - Jewish American literature
    - Southern literature
  - Australian literature
  - British literature (literature from some regions of the United Kingdom may be written in Celtic languages)
  - Canadian literature (a significant amount of Canadian literature is also written in French)
  - Irish literature
  - New Zealand literature
  - Scottish literature
  - Welsh literature

2

English Language: Origin and Development

Basically, English is a West Germanic language originating in England, and is the first language for most people in the Anglophone Caribbean, Australia, Canada, New Zealand, the Republic of Ireland, the United Kingdom, and the United States (sometimes referred to as the Anglosphere). It is used extensively as a second language and as an official language throughout the world, especially in Commonwealth countries and in many international organisations. A native or fluent speaker of English is known as an Anglophone.

Modern English is sometimes described as the first global lingua franca. English is the dominant international language in communications, science, business, aviation, entertainment, radio and diplomacy. The influence of the British Empire is the primary reason for the initial spread of the language far beyond the British Isles. Since World War II, the growing economic and cultural influence of the United States has significantly accelerated the adoption of English.

English is an Anglo-Frisian language. Germanic-speaking peoples from northwest Germany (Saxons and

Angles) and Jutland (Jutes) invaded what is now known as Eastern England around the fifth century AD. It is a matter of debate whether the Old English language spread by displacement of the original population, or the native Celts gradually adopted the language and culture of a new ruling class, or a combination of both of these processes.

Whatever their origin, these Germanic dialects eventually coalesced to a degree (there remained geographical variation) and formed what is today called Old English. Old English loosely resembles some coastal dialects in what are now northwest Germany and the Netherlands (i.e., Frisia). Throughout the history of written Old English, it retained a synthetic structure closer to that of Proto-Indo-European, largely adopting West Saxon scribal conventions, while spoken Old English became increasingly analytic in nature, losing the more complex noun case system, relying more heavily on prepositions and fixed word order to convey meaning. This is evident in the Middle English period, when literature was to an increasing extent recorded with spoken dialectal variation intact, after written Old English lost its status as the literary language of the nobility. It has been postulated that English retains some traits from a Celtic substratum.

Later, it was influenced by the related North Germanic language Old Norse, spoken by the Vikings who settled mainly in the north and the east coast down to London, the area known as the Danelaw. The Norman Conquest of England in 1066 greatly influenced the evolution of the language. For about 300 years after this, the Normans used Anglo-Norman, which was close to Old French, as the language of the court, law and administration. By the latter part of the fourteenth century, when English had replaced French as the language of law and government,

Anglo-Norman borrowings had contributed roughly 10,000 words to English, of which 75% remain in use. These include many words pertaining to the legal and administrative fields, but also include common words for food, such as mutton, beef, and pork. However, the animals associated with these foods (e.g. sheep, cow, and swine) retained their Saxon names, possibly because as a herd animal they were tended by Saxon serfs, while as food, they were more likely to be consumed at a Norman table.

The Norman influence heavily influenced what is now referred to as Middle English. Later, during the English Renaissance, many words were borrowed directly from Latin (giving rise to a number of doublets) and Greek, leaving a parallel vocabulary that persists into modern times. By the seventeenth century there was a reaction in some circles against so-called *inkhorn terms*.

During the fifteenth century, Middle English was transformed by the Great Vowel Shift, the spread of a prestigious South Eastern-based dialect in the court, administration and academic life, and the standardising effect of printing. Early Modern English can be traced back to around the Elizabethan period.

Classification and Related Languages

Though English language belongs to the western sub-branch of the Germanic branch of the Indo-European family of languages, the question as to which is the nearest living relative of English is a matter of discussion. Apart from such English-lexified creole languages such as Tok Pisin, Scots (spoken primarily in Scotland and parts of Northern Ireland) is not a Gaelic language, but is part of the Anglic family of languages, having developed from early northern Middle English. It is Scots' indefinite status as a language or a group of dialects of English which complicates definitely calling it the closest language to English.

The closest relatives to English after Scots are the Frisian languages, which are spoken in the Northern Netherlands and Northwest Germany. Other less closely related living West Germanic languages include German, Low Saxon, Dutch, and Afrikaans. The North Germanic languages of Scandinavia are less closely related to English than the West Germanic languages. Many French words are also intelligible to an English speaker (though pronunciations are often quite different) because English absorbed a large vocabulary from Norman and French, via Anglo-Norman after the Norman Conquest and directly from French in subsequent centuries. As a result, a large portion of English vocabulary is derived from French, with some minor spelling differences (word endings, use of old French spellings, etc.), as well as occasional divergences in meaning, in so-called "faux amis", or false friends.

Geographical Distribution

Approximately 375 million people speak English as their first language, as of 2006. English today is probably the third largest language by number of native speakers, after Mandarin Chinese and Spanish. However, when combining native and non-native speakers it is probably the most commonly spoken language in the world, though possibly second to a combination of the Chinese Languages, depending on whether or not distinctions in the latter are classified as "languages" or "dialects." Estimates that include second language speakers vary greatly from 470 million to over a billion depending on how literacy or mastery is defined. There are some who claim that non-native speakers now outnumber native speakers by a ratio of 3 to 1.

The countries with the highest populations of native English speakers are, in descending order: United States (215 million), United Kingdom (58 million), Canada (17.7 million), Australia (15.5 million), Ireland (3.8 million), South Africa (3.7 million), and New Zealand (3.0-3.7 million). Countries such as Jamaica and Nigeria also have millions of native speakers of dialect continua ranging from an English-based creole to a more standard version of English. Of those nations where English is spoken as a second language, India has the most such speakers ('Indian English') and linguistics professor David Crystal claims that, combining native and non-native speakers, India now has more people who speak or understand English than any other country in the world. Following India is the People's Republic of China.

English is the primary language in Anguilla, Antigua and Barbuda, Australia (Australian English), the Bahamas, Barbados, Bermuda, Belize, the British Indian Ocean Territory, the British Virgin Islands, Canada (Canadian English), the Cayman Islands, the Falkland Islands, Gibraltar, Grenada, Guam, Guernsey (Guernsey English), Guyana, Ireland (Hiberno-English), Isle of Man (Manx English), Jamaica (Jamaican English), Jersey, Montserrat, Nauru, New Zealand (New Zealand English), Pitcairn Islands, Saint Helena, Saint Kitts and Nevis, Saint Vincent and the Grenadines, South Georgia and the South Sandwich Islands, Trinidad and Tobago, the Turks and Caicos Islands, the United Kingdom, the U.S. Virgin Islands, and the United States (various forms of American English).

In many other countries, where English is not the most spoken language, it is an official language; these countries include Botswana, Cameroon, Dominica, Fiji, the Federated States of Micronesia, Ghana, Gambia, India,

Kiribati, Lesotho, Liberia, Kenya, Madagascar, Malta, the Marshall Islands, Mauritius, Namibia, Nigeria, Pakistan, Palau, Papua New Guinea, the Philippines, Puerto Rico, Rwanda, the Solomon Islands, Saint Lucia, Samoa, Seychelles, Sierra Leone, Singapore, Sri Lanka, Swaziland, Tanzania, Uganda, Zambia, and Zimbabwe. It is also one of the 11 official languages that are given equal status in South Africa (South African English). English is also the official language in current dependent territories of Australia (Norfolk Island, Christmas Island and Cocos Island) and of the United States (Northern Mariana Islands, American Samoa and Puerto Rico), and in the former British colony of Hong Kong.

English is an important language in several former colonies and protectorates of the United Kingdom but falls short of official status, such as in Malaysia, Brunei, United Arab Emirates and Bahrain. English is also not an official language in either the United States or the United Kingdom. Although the United States federal government has no official languages, English has been given official status by 30 of the 50 state governments.

English as a Global Language

Because English is so widely spoken, it has often been referred to as a "global language", the *lingua franca* of the modern era. While English is not an official language in most countries, it is currently the language most often taught as a second language around the world. Some linguists believe that it is no longer the exclusive cultural sign of "native English speakers", but is rather a language that is absorbing aspects of cultures worldwide as it continues to grow. It is, by international treaty, the official language for aerial and maritime communications, as well as one of the official languages of the European Union, the

United Nations, and most international athletic organisations, including the International Olympic Committee.

English is the language most often studied as a foreign language in the European Union (by 89% of schoolchildren), followed by French (32%), German (18%), and Spanish (8%). In the EU, a large fraction of the population reports being able to converse to some extent in English. Among non-English speaking countries, a large percentage of the population claimed to be able to converse in English in the Netherlands (87%), Sweden (85%), Denmark (83%), Luxembourg (66%), Finland (60%), Slovenia (56%), Austria (53%), Belgium (52%), and Germany (51%). Norway and Iceland also have a large majority of competent English-speakers.

Books, magazines, and newspapers written in English are available in many countries around the world. English is also the most commonly used language in the sciences. In 1997, the Science Citation Index reported that 95% of its articles were written in English, even though only half of them came from authors in English-speaking countries.

Dialects and Regional Varieties

The expansion of the British Empire and—since WWII—the primacy of the United States have spread English throughout the globe. Because of that global spread, English has developed a host of English dialects and English-based creole languages and pidgins.

The major varieties of English include, in most cases, several subvarieties, such as Cockney slang within British English; Newfoundland English within Canadian English; and African American Vernacular English ("Ebonics") and Southern American English within American English.

English is a pluricentric language, without a central language authority like France's Académie française; and, although no variety is clearly considered the only standard, there are a number of accents considered to be more prestigious, such as Received Pronunciation in Britain.

Scots developed — largely independently — from the same origins, but following the Acts of Union 1707 a process of language attrition began, whereby successive generations adopted more and more features from English causing dialectalisation. Whether it is now a separate language or a dialect of English better described as Scottish English is in dispute. The pronunciation, grammar and lexis of the traditional forms differ, sometimes substantially, from other varieties of English.

Because of the wide use of English as a second language, English speakers have many different accents, which often signal the speaker's native dialect or language. For the more distinctive characteristics of regional accents, see Regional accents of English speakers, and for the more distinctive characteristics of regional dialects, see List of dialects of the English language.

Just as English itself has borrowed words from many different languages over its history, English loanwords now appear in a great many languages around the world, indicative of the technological and cultural influence of its speakers. Several pidgins and creole languages have formed using an English base, such as Jamaican Creole, Nigerian Pidgin, and Tok Pisin. There are many words in English coined to describe forms of particular non-English languages that contain a very high proportion of English words. Franglais, for example, is used to describe French with a very high English word content; it is found on the Channel

Islands. Another variant, spoken in the border bilingual regions of Québec in Canada, is called Frenglish.

Constructed Varieties of English

- Basic English is simplified for easy international use. It is used by manufacturers and other international businesses to write manuals and communicate. Some English schools in Asia teach it as a practical subset of English for use by beginners.
- Special English is a simplified version of English used by the Voice of America. It uses a vocabulary of only 1500 words.
- English reform is an attempt to improve collectively upon the English language.
- Seaspeak and the related Airspeak and Policespeak, all based on restricted vocabularies, were designed by Edward Johnson in the 1980s to aid international cooperation and communication in specific areas. There is also a tunnelspeak for use in the Channel Tunnel.
- Euro-English is a concept of standardising English for use as a second language in continental Europe.
- Manually Coded English — a variety of systems have been developed to represent the English language with hand signals, designed primarily for use in deaf education. These should not be confused with true sign languages such as British Sign Language and American Sign Language used in Anglophone countries, which are independent and not based on English.
- E-Prime excludes forms of the verb *to be*.

Euro-English (also *EuroEnglish* or *Euro-English*) terms are English translations of European concepts that are not native to English-speaking countries. Because of the United Kingdom's (and even the Republic of Ireland's) involvement in the European Union, the usage focuses on non-British concepts. This kind of Euro-English was parodied when English was "made" one of the constituent languages of Europanto.

Phonology

It is the vowels that differ most from region to region.

Where symbols appear in pairs, the first corresponds to American English, General American accent; the second corresponds to British English, Received Pronunciation.

1. American English lacks this sound; words with this sound are pronounced with /Q/ or /T/.

2. Many dialects of North American English do not have this vowel. See *Cot-caught merger*.

3. The North American variation of this sound is a rhotic vowel.

4. Many speakers of North American English do not distinguish between these two unstressed vowels. For them, *roses* and *Rosa's* are pronounced the same, and the symbol usually used is schwa /Y/.

5. This sound is often transcribed with /i/ or with /j/.

6. The diphthongs /ej/ and /oŠ/ are monophthongal for many General American speakers, as /eÐ/ and /oÐ/.

7. The letter <*U*> can represent either /u/ or the iotated vowel /ju/. In BRP, if this iotated vowel /ju/ occurs after /t/ , /d/, /s/ or /z/, it often triggers palatalization of the preceding

consonant, turning it to /'/, /¥/, /U/ and /'/ respectively, as in *tune*, *during*, *sugar*, and *azure*. In American English, palatalization does not generally happen unless the /ju/ is followed by *r*, with the result that /(t, d,s, z)jur/ turn to / tfZ/, /d'Z/, /fZ/ and /'Z/ respectively, as in *nature*, *verdure*, *sure*, and *treasure*.

8. Vowel length plays a phonetic role in the majority of English dialects, and is said to be phonemic in a few dialects, such as Australian English and New Zealand English. In certain dialects of the modern English language, for instance General American, there is allophonic vowel length: vowel phonemes are realized as long vowel allophones before voiced consonant phonemes in the coda of a syllable. Before the Great Vowel Shift, vowel length was phonemically contrastive.

9. This sound only occurs in non-rhotic accents. In some accents, this sound may be, instead of /ŠY/, /T:/. See pour-poor merger.

10. This sound only occurs in non-rhotic accents. In some accents, the schwa offglide of /[Y/ may be dropped, monophthising and lengthening the sound to /[:/.

Consonants

This is the English Consonantal System using symbols from the International Phonetic Alphabet (IPA).

1. The velar nasal [K] is a non-phonemic allophone of /n/ in some northerly British accents, appearing only before /k/ and /g/. In all other dialects it is a separate phoneme, although it only occurs in syllable codas.

2. The alveolar flap [~] is an allophone of /t/ and /d/ in unstressed syllables in North American English and Australian English. This is the sound of *tt* or *dd* in the

words *latter* and *ladder*, which are homophones for many speakers of North American English. In some accents such as Scottish English and Indian English it replaces /y/. This is the same sound represented by single *r* in most varieties of Spanish.

3. In some dialects, such as Cockney, the interdentals /è/ and /ð/ are usually merged with /f/ and /v/, and in others, like African American Vernacular English, /ð/ is merged with dental /d/. In some Irish varieties, /è/ and /ð/ become the corresponding dental plosives, which then contrast with the usual alveolar plosives.

4. The sounds /*f*/, /'/, and /y/ are labialised in some dialects. Labialisation is never contrastive in initial position and therefore is sometimes not transcribed. Most speakers of General American realize <r> (always rhoticized) as the retroflex approximant /{/, whereas the same is realized in Scottish English, etc. as the alveolar trill.

5. The voiceless palatal fricative /ç/ is in most accents just an allophone of /h/ before /j/; for instance *human* /çjuÐmYn/. However, in some accents (see this), the /j/ is dropped, but the initial consonant is the same.

6. The voiceless velar fricative /x/ is used by Scottish or Welsh speakers of English for Scots/Gaelic words such as *loch* /lRx/ or by some speakers for loanwords from German and Hebrew like *Bach* /bax/ or *Chanukah* /xanuka/. /x/ is also used in South African English. In some dialects such as Scouse (Liverpool) either [x] or the affricate [kx] may be used as an allophone of /k/ in words such as *docker* [dRkxY]. Most native speakers have a great deal of trouble pronouncing it correctly when learning a foreign language. Most speakers use the sounds [k] and [h] instead.

7. Voiceless w [•] is found in Scottish and Irish English, as well as in some varieties of American, New Zealand, and English English. In most other dialects it is merged with /w/, in some dialects of Scots it is merged with /f/.

Voicing and Aspiration

Voicing and aspiration of stop consonants in English depend on dialect and context, but a few general rules can be given:

- Voiceless plosives and affricates (/ p/, / t/, / k/, and / tʃ/) are aspirated when they are word-initial or begin a stressed syllable — compare *pin* [p°jn] and *spin* [spjn], *crap* and *scrap* [skyæp].
  - In some dialects, aspiration extends to unstressed syllables as well.
  - In other dialects, such as Indo-Pakistani English, all voiceless stops remain unaspirated.
- Word-initial voiced plosives may be devoiced in some dialects.
- Word-terminal voiceless plosives may be unreleased or accompanied by a glottal stop in some dialects (e.g. many varieties of American English) — examples: *tap* [t°æp], *sack* [sæk].
- Word-terminal voiced plosives may be devoiced in some dialects (e.g. some varieties of American English) — examples: *sad* [sæd%], *bag* [bæa]. In other dialects they are fully voiced in final position, but only partially voiced in initial position.

Supra-segmental Features

Tone Groups

English is an intonation language. This means that

the pitch of the voice is used syntactically, for example, to convey surprise and irony, or to change a statement into a question.

In English, intonation patterns are on groups of words, which are called tone groups, tone units, intonation groups or sense groups. Tone groups are said on a single breath and, as a consequence, are of limited length, more often being on average five words long or lasting roughly two seconds.

Characteristics of Intonation

English is a strongly stressed language, in that certain syllables, both within words and within phrases, get a relative prominence/loudness during pronunciation while the others do not. The former kind of syllables are said to be *accentuated / stressed* and the latter are *unaccentuated / unstressed*. All good dictionaries of English mark the accentuated syllable(s) by either placing an apostrophe-like (È) sign either before (as in IPA, Oxford English Dictionary, or Merriam-Webster dictionaries) or after (as in many other dictionaries) the syllable where the stress accent falls.

Hence in a sentence, each tone group can be subdivided into syllables, which can either be stressed (strong) or unstressed (weak). The stressed syllable is called the nuclear syllable. For example:

That | was | the | best | thing | you | could | have | done!

Here, all syllables are unstressed, except the syllables/words *best* and *done*, which are stressed. *Best* is stressed harder and, therefore, is the nuclear syllable.

The nuclear syllable carries the main point the speaker wishes to make. For example:

John had not stolen that money. (... Someone else had.)

John *had not* stolen that money. (... You said he had. or ... Not at that time, but later he did.)

John had not *stolen* that money. (... He acquired the money by some other means.)

John had not stolen *that* money. (... He had stolen some other money.)

John had not stolen that *money*. (... He stole something else.)

Also

I did not tell her that. (... Someone else told her)

I *did not* tell her that. (... You said I did. or ... but now I will)

I did not *tell* her that. (... I did not say it; she could have inferred it, etc)

I did not tell *her* that. (... I told someone else)

I did not tell her *that*. (... I told her something else)

This can also be used to express emotion:

Oh really? (...I did not know that)

Oh *really*? (...I disbelieve you. or ... That's blatantly obvious)

The nuclear syllable is spoken more loudly than the

others and has a characteristic change of pitch. The changes of pitch most commonly encountered in English are the rising pitch and the falling pitch, although the fall-rising pitch and/or the rise-falling pitch are sometimes used. In this opposition between falling and rising pitch, which plays a larger role in English than in most other languages, falling pitch conveys certainty and rising pitch uncertainty. This can have a crucial impact on meaning, specifically in relation to polarity, the positive–negative opposition; thus, falling pitch means "polarity known", while rising pitch means "polarity unknown". This underlies the rising pitch of yes/no questions. For example:

> *When do you want to be paid?*
>
> *Now?* (Rising pitch. In this case, it denotes a question: "Can I be paid now?" or "Do you desire to be paid now?")
>
> *Now.* (Falling pitch. In this case, it denotes a statement: "I choose to be paid now.")

Grammar

English grammar has minimal inflection compared with most other Indo-European languages. For example, Modern English, unlike Modern German or Dutch and the Romance languages, lacks grammatical gender and adjectival agreement. Case marking has almost disappeared from the language and mainly survives in pronouns. The patterning of strong (e.g. *speak / spoke / spoken*) versus weak verbs inherited from its Germanic origins has declined in importance in modern English, and the remnants of inflection (such as plural marking) have become more regular. At the same time, the language has become more analytic, and has developed features such as modal verbs and word order as rich resources for conveying meaning. Auxiliary verbs mark constructions such as questions, negative polarity, the passive voice and progressive aspect.

Vocabulary

The English vocabulary has changed considerably over the centuries. Like many languages deriving from Proto-Indo-European (PIE), many of the most common words in English can trace back their origin (through Germanic) to PIE. Such words include the basic pronouns I, originally *ic*, (cf. Latin *ego*, Greek *ego*, Sanskrit *aham*), *me* (cf. Latin *me*, Greek *eme*, Sanskrit *mam*), numbers (e.g. *one*, *two*, *three*, cf. Latin *unus, duo, tres*, Greek *oios, duo, treis*), common family relationships such as mother, father, brother, sister etc (cf. Greek "meter", Latin "mater", Sanskrit "mat["; *mother*), names of many animals (cf. Sankrit *mus*, Greek *mys*, Latin *mus*; *mouse*), and many common verbs (cf. Greek *gignômi*, Latin *gnoscere*, Hittite *kanes;to know*).

Germanic words (generally words of Old English or to a lesser extent Norse origin) tend to be shorter than the Latinate words of English, and more common in ordinary speech. This includes nearly all the basic pronouns, prepositions, conjunctions, modals etc. that form the basis of English syntax and grammar. The longer Latinate words are often regarded as more elegant or educated. However, the excessive use of Latinate words is considered at times to be either pretentious (as in the stereotypical policeman's talk of "apprehending the suspect") or an attempt to obfuscate an issue. George Orwell's essay "Politics and the English Language" is critical of this, as well as other perceived abuses of the language. An English speaker is in many cases able to choose between Germanic and Latinate synonyms: *come* or *arrive*; *sight* or *vision*; *freedom* or *liberty*.

In some cases there is a choice between a Germanic

derived word (*oversee*), a Latin derived word (*supervise*), and a French word derived from the same Latin word (*survey*). The richness of the language arises from the variety of different meanings and nuances such synonyms harbour, enabling the speaker to express fine variations or shades of thought. Familiarity with the etymology of groups of synonyms can give English speakers greater control over their linguistic register. An exception to this and a peculiarity perhaps unique to English is that the nouns for meats are commonly different from, and unrelated to, those for the animals from which they are produced, the animal commonly having a Germanic name and the meat having a French-derived one.

Examples include: *deer* and *venison*; *cow* and *beef*; *swine/pig* and *pork*, or *sheep* and *mutton*. This is assumed to be a result of the aftermath of the Norman invasion, where a French-speaking elite were the consumers of the meat, produced by Anglo-Saxon lower classes.

Since the majority of words used in informal settings will normally be Germanic, such words are often the preferred choices when a speaker wishes to make a point in an argument in a very direct way. A majority of Latinate words (or at least a majority of content words) will normally be used in more formal speech and writing, such as a courtroom or an encyclopedia article. However, there are other Latinate words that are used normally in everyday speech and do not sound formal; these are mainly words for concepts that no longer have Germanic words, and are generally assimilated better and in many cases do not appear Latinate.

For instance, the words *mountain*, *valley*, *river*, *aunt*, *uncle*, *move*, *use*, *push* and *stay* are all Latinate. English easily accepts technical terms into common usage and often imports new words and phrases. Examples of this phenomenon include: *cookie*, *Internet* and *URL* (technical terms), as well as *genre*, *über*, *lingua franca* and *amigo* (imported words/phrases from French, German, modern Latin, and Spanish, respectively).

In addition, slang often provides new meanings for old words and phrases. In fact, this fluidity is so pronounced that a distinction often needs to be made between formal forms of English and contemporary usage.

Number of Words in English

English has an extraordinarily rich vocabulary and capacity to absorb and create new words. As the *General Explanations* at the beginning of the *Oxford English Dictionary* states:

> "The Vocabulary of a widely diffused and highly cultivated living language is not a fixed quantity circumscribed by definite limits... there is absolutely no defining line in any direction: the circle of the English language has a well-defined centre but no discernible circumference."

The vocabulary of English is undoubtedly vast, but assigning a specific number to its size is more a matter of definition than of calculation. Unlike other languages, such as French, German, Spanish and Italian there is no Academy to define officially accepted words and spellings. Neologisms are coined regularly in medicine, science and technology and other fields, and new slang is constantly developed. Some of these new words enter wide usage; others remain restricted to small circles. Foreign words used in immigrant communities often make their way into wider English usage. Archaic, dialectal, and regional words might or might not be widely considered as "English".

The *Oxford English Dictionary,* 2nd edition *(OED2)* includes over 600,000 definitions, following a rather inclusive policy:

> "It embraces not only the standard language of literature and conversation, whether current at the moment, or obsolete, or archaic, but also the main technical vocabulary, and a large measure of dialectal usage and slang (Supplement to the *OED,* 1933)."

The editors of *Webster's Third New International Dictionary, Unabridged* (475,000 main headwords) in their preface, estimate the number to be much higher. It is estimated that about 25,000 words are added to the language each year.

Word Origins

One of the consequences of the French influence is that the vocabulary of English is, to a certain extent, divided between those words which are Germanic (mostly West Germanic, with a smaller influence from the North Germanic branch) and those which are "Latinate" (Latin-derived, either directly from Norman French or other Romance languages).

Numerous sets of statistics have been proposed to demonstrate the origins of English vocabulary. None, as yet, is considered definitive by most linguists.

A computerised survey of about 80,000 words in the old *Shorter Oxford Dictionary* (3rd ed.) was published in *Ordered Profusion* by Thomas Finkenstaedt and Dieter Wolff (1973) that estimated the origin of English words as follows:

- *Langue d'oïl*, including French and Old Norman: 28.3%
- Latin, including modern scientific and technical Latin: 28.24%
- Other Germanic languages (including words directly inherited from Old English): 25%
- Greek: 5.32%
- No etymology given: 4.03%
- Derived from proper names: 3.28%
- All other languages contributed less than 1% (e.g. Arabic-English loanwords)

A survey by Joseph M. Williams in *Origins of the English Language* of 10,000 words taken from several thousand business letters gave this set of statistics:

- French (langue d'oïl), 41%
- "Native" English, 33%
- Latin, 15%
- Danish, 2%
- Dutch, 1%
- Other, 10%

However, 83% of the 1,000 most-common, and all of the 100 most-common English words are Germanic.

Dutch Origins

Words describing the navy, types of ships, and other objects or activities on the water are often from Dutch origin. *Yacht* (*jacht*) and *cruiser* (*kruiser*) are examples.

French Origins

There are many words of French origin in English,

such as *competition, art, table, publicity, police, role, routine, machine, force*, and many others that have been and are being anglicised; they are now pronounced according to English rules of phonology, rather than French. A large portion of English vocabulary is of French or Oïl language origin, most derived from, or transmitted via, the Anglo-Norman spoken by the upper classes in England for several hundred years after the Norman Conquest.

Writing System

English has been written using the Latin alphabet since around the ninth century. (Before that, Old English had been written using the Anglo-Saxon Futhorc.) The spelling system, or orthography, is multilayered, with elements of French, Latin and Greek spelling on top of the native Germanic system; it has grown to vary significantly from the phonology of the language. The spelling of words often diverges considerably from how they are spoken..

Though letters and sounds may not correspond in isolation, spelling rules that take into account syllable structure, phonetics, and accents are 75% or more reliable. Some phonics spelling advocates claim that English is more than 80% phonetic.

Generally, the English language, being the product of many other languages and having only been codified orthographically in the 16th century, has fewer consistent relationships between sounds and letters than many other languages. The consequence of this orthographic history is that reading can be challenging. It takes longer for students to become completely fluent readers of English than of many other languages, including French, Greek, and Spanish.

Written Accents

Unlike most other Germanic languages, English has almost no diacritics, except in foreign loanwords (like the acute accent in *café*) and in the uncommon use of a diaeresis mark (often in formal writing) to indicate that two vowels are pronounced separately, rather than as one sound (e.g. *naïve, Zoë*). In most cases it is acceptable to leave out the marks, especially in digital communications where the QWERTY keyboard lacks any marked letters.

Formal Written English

A version of the language almost universally agreed upon by educated English speakers around the world is called formal written English. It takes virtually the same form no matter where in the English-speaking world it is written. In spoken English, by contrast, there are a vast number of differences between dialects, accents, and varieties of slang, colloquial and regional expressions. In spite of this, local variations in the formal written version of the language are quite limited, being restricted largely to the spelling differences between British and American English.

Basic and Simplified Versions

To make English easier to read, there are some simplified versions of the language. One basic version is named *Basic English*, a constructed language with a small number of words created by Charles Kay Ogden and described in his book *Basic English: A General Introduction with Rules and Grammar* (1930). The language is based on a simplified version of English. Ogden said that it would take seven years to learn English, seven months for Esperanto, and seven weeks for Basic English, comparable with Ido. Thus Basic English is used by companies who need to make complex books for international use, and by language schools that need to give people some knowledge of English in a short time.

Ogden did not put any words into Basic English that could be said with a few other words and he worked to make the words work for speakers of any other language. He put his set of words through a large number of tests and adjustments. He also made the grammar simpler, but tried to keep the grammar normal for English users.

The concept gained its greatest publicity just after the Second World War as a tool for world peace. Although it was not built into a program, similar simplifications were devised for various international uses.

Another version, Simplified English, exists, which is a controlled language originally developed for aerospace industry maintenance manuals. It offers a carefully limited and standardised subset of English. Simplified English has a lexicon of approved words and those words can only be used in certain ways. For example, the word *close* can be used in the phrase "Close the door" but not "do not go close to the landing gear".

II

MIDDLE ENGLISH CREOLE HYPOTHESIS

The Middle English creole hypothesis is the conjecture that the English language is a creole, i.e., a language that developed from a pidgin. The vast differences between Old and Middle English have led some historical linguists to claim that the language underwent creolisation at the time of either the Norse or Norman Conquests, or during both.

Differences between Middle and Old English

The argument in favour of calling Middle English a creole comes from the extreme reduction in inflected forms from Old English to Middle English. The system of declension of nouns was radically simplified and analogised. The verb system also lost many old patterns of conjugation. Many strong verbs were reanalyzed as weak verbs. The subjunctive mood became much less distinct. Syntax was also simplified somewhat, with word order patterns becoming more rigid.

These grammatical simplifications resemble those observed in pidgins, creoles, and other contact languages, which arise when speakers of two different languages need to communicate with one another. Such contact languages usually lack the inflections of either parent language, or drastically simplify them. However, many say that English is probably not a creole because it retains a high number (283) of irregular verbs.

It is certain that English underwent grammatical changes, e.g., the collapse of all cases into genitive and common. However, the reduction of unstressed vowels to schwa due to a fixed stress location contributed to this process, a pattern common to many Germanic languages (although several, such as dialects of Norwegian, Icelandic, and Faroese, have not undergone the reduction of vowel sounds). The process of case collapse was also already underway in Old English. For example, in strong masculine nouns, the nominative and accusative cases had become identical. Thus, the simplification of noun declension from Old English to Middle English may have had causes unrelated to creolisation.

French Influences

No one can deny with validity that English had an

unusual amount of French and Norman loanwords. However, most of the borrowing happened after 1400, two centuries after the nobility ceased to be French speaking. The most striking Norse borrowing, their pronouns, cannot be attributed to creolisation either. It was more likely a result of ambiguity between *hiem* and *him* etc.

Most Romance languages have only two grammatical genders, *masculine* and *feminine*. Most Germanic languages have *masculine*, *feminine*, and *neuter*. It has been suggested that since these two gender systems are incompatible, English responded by dropping genders altogether, but this is only conjecture. The loss of agreement between modifiers is perhaps attributable to the reduction to schwa.

The plural form in English originates from a masculine nominative-accusative plural (Old English *-as*) and is cognate with the Old Saxon plural *-os* and the Old Norse plural *-ar*. The French plural descends from oblique formations in Old French and is ultimately of pronominal, not nominal origin so the plural forms in the two languages are not related. There is at least one change that may be a direct result of French influence: the loss of *Thou*. Under Norman influence, *Thou* came to be parallel with *Tu*. Due to politeness among English speakers, *Thou* fell into disuse. However, a similar process took place across Western Europe, including Spain and Germany; see T-V distinction.

The combination of a largely French speaking aristocracy and a largely English speaking peasantry gave rise to many pairs of words with a Latinate word in the higher register and a Germanic word in the lower register. For example, the names of barnyard animals tend to be Germanic, from the names the English farmers and herders used:

- chicken
- calf
- cow
- sheep
- swine

The names of the animals when they appear on one's plate, as the aristocracy saw them, are of Latin origin:

- poultry
- veal
- beef
- mutton
- pork

Other such doublets include:

Origin

Latin	Germanic
Bellicose	warlike
benediction	blessing
Close	shut
commence	begin
decapitate	behead
Desire	wish
Gentle	mild
Labour	work
Novel	new
Verity	truth

During the reign of the Normans, many words related to the ruling classes and the business of government entered English from French. Among these words are:

- attorney
- bailiff
- baron
- city
- conservative
- countess
- county
- damage
- duchess
- duke
- empire
- executive
- felony
- govern
- judicial
- jury
- justice
- legislative
- liberal
- marriage
- nobility
- parliament
- perjury
- petty
- prince
- prison
- regal

- representative
- republic
- royal
- senator
- sovereign
- state
- traitor
- viscount

A few words retain the French construction of noun followed by adjective, in contrast to the typical English construction of adjective plus noun:

- attorney general
- court martial
- malice aforethought

III

ENGLISH LANGUAGE LEARNING AND TEACHING

ESL (English as a second language), ESOL (English for speakers of other languages), and EFL (English as a foreign language) all refer to the use or study of English by speakers with a different native language. The precise usage, including the different use of the terms ESL and ESOL in different countries, is described below. These terms are most commonly used in relation to teaching and learning English, but they may also be used in relation to demographic information.

ELT (English language teaching) is a widely-used teacher-centred term, as in the English language teaching divisions of large publishing houses, ELT training, etc.

The abbreviations TESL (teaching English as a second language), TESOL (teaching English for speakers of other languages) and TEFL (teaching English as a foreign language) are all also used.

Other terms used in this field include EAL (English as an additional language), ESD (English as a second dialect), EIL (English as an international language), ELF (English as a lingua franca), ESP (English for special purposes, or English for specific purposes), EAP (English for academic purposes). Some terms that refer to those who are learning English are ELL (English language learner), LEP (limited English proficiency) and CLD (culturally and linguistically diverse).

Terminology and Types

The many acronyms used in the field of English teaching and learning may be confusing. English is a language with great reach and influence; it is taught all over the world under many different circumstances. In English-speaking countries, English language teaching has essentially evolved in two broad directions: instruction for people who intend to stay in the country and those who don't. These divisions have grown firmer as the instructors of these two "industries" have used different terminology, followed distinct training qualifications, formed separate professional associations, and so on. Crucially, these two arms have very different funding structures, public in the former and private in the latter, and to some extent this influences the way schools are established and classes are held. Matters are further complicated by the fact that the United States and the United Kingdom, both major engines of the language, describe these categories in different terms: as many eloquent users of the language have observed, "England and America are two countries divided by a common language."

(Attributed to Winston Churchill, George Bernard Shaw, and Oscar Wilde.) The following technical definitions may therefore have their currency contested.

English Outside English-speaking Countries

EFL, English as a foreign language, indicates the use of English in a non-English-speaking region. Study can occur either in the student's home country, as part of the normal school curriculum or otherwise, or, for the more privileged minority, in an anglophone country that they visit as a sort of educational tourist, particularly immediately before or after graduating from university. *TEFL* is the teaching of English as a foreign language; note that this sort of instruction can take place in any country, English-speaking or not.

Typically, EFL is learned either to pass exams as a necessary part of one's education, or for career progression while working for an organisation or business with an international focus. EFL may be part of the state school curriculum in countries where English has no special status (what linguist Braj Kachru calls the "expanding circle countries"); it may also be supplemented by lessons paid for privately. Teachers of EFL generally assume that students are literate in their mother tongue. The Chinese EFL Journal and Iranian EFL Journal are examples of international journals dedicated to specifics of English language learning within countries where English is used as a foreign language.

English within English-speaking Countries

The other broad grouping is the use of English within the Anglosphere. In what theorist Braj Kachru calls "the inner circle", i.e. countries such as the United Kingdom and the United States, this use of English is generally by refugees, immigrants and their children. It also includes the use of English in "outer circle" countries, often former British colonies, where English is an official language even if it is not spoken as a mother tongue by the majority of the population.

In the US, Canada and Australia, this use of English is called *ESL* (English as a second language). This term has been criticized on the grounds that many learners already speak more than one language. A counter-argument says that the word "a" in the phrase "a second language" means there is no presumption that English is *the* second acquired language. *TESL* is the teaching of English as a second language.

In the UK, Ireland and New Zealand, the term ESL has been replaced by *ESOL* (English for speakers of other languages). In these countries *TESOL* (teaching English to speakers of other languages) is normally used to refer to teaching English only to this group. In the UK, the term *EAL* (English as an additional language), rather than ESOL, is usually used when talking about primary and secondary schools.

Other acronyms were created to describe the person rather than the language to be learned. The term LEP (Limited English proficiency) was created in 1975 by the Lau Remedies following a decision of the US Supreme Court. ELL (English Language Learner), used by United States governments and school systems, was created by Charlene Rivera of the Center for Equity and Excellent in Education in an effort to label learners positively, rather than ascribing a deficiency to them. LOTE (Languages other than English) is a parallel term used in Canada, Australia, and New Zealand.

Typically, this sort of English (called ESL in the United States, Canada, and Australia, ESOL in the United Kingdom, Ireland and New Zealand) is learned to function in the new host country, e.g. within the school system (if a child), to find and hold down a job (if an adult), to perform the necessities of daily life. The teaching of it does not presuppose literacy in the mother tongue. It is usually paid for by the host government to help newcomers settle into their adopted country, sometimes as part of an explicit citizenship program. It is technically possible for ESL to be taught not in the host country, but in, for example, a refugee camp, as part of a pre-departure program sponsored by the government soon to receive new potential citizens. In practice, however, this is extremely rare.

Particularly in Canada and Australia, the term *ESD* (English as a second dialect) is used alongside ESL, usually in reference to programs for Canadian First Nations people or indigenous Australians, respectively. It refers to the use of standard English, which may need to be explicitly taught, by speakers of a creole or non-standard variety. It is often grouped with ESL as *ESL/ESD*.

Umbrella Terms

All these ways of teaching English can be bundled together into an umbrella term. Unfortunately, all the English teachers in the world cannot agree on just one. The term *TESOL* (teaching English to speakers of other languages) is used in American English to include both TEFL and TESL. British English uses *ELT* (English language teaching), because TESOL has a different, more specific meaning; see above.

Which Variety to Teach

It is worth noting that ESL and EFL programs also

differ in the variety of English which is taught; "English" is a term that can refer to various dialects, including British English, American English, and many others. Obviously, those studying English in order to fit into their new country will learn the variety spoken there. However, for those who do not intend to change countries, the question arises of which sort of English to learn. If they are going abroad for a short time to study English, they need to choose which country. For those staying at home, the choice may be made for them in that private language schools or the state school system may only offer one model. Students studying EFL in Hong Kong, for example, are more likely to learn British English, whereas students in the Philippines are more likely to learn American English.

For this reason, many teachers now emphasize teaching English as an international language (EIL), also known as English as a -lingua franca (ELF). Linguists are charting the development of international English, a term with contradictory and confusing meanings, one of which refers to a decontextualised variant of the language, independent of the culture and associated references of any particular country, useful when, for example, a Saudi does business with someone from China or Albania.

Systems of Simplified English

For international communication several models of "simplified English" have been suggested, among them:

- Basic English, developed by Charles Kay Ogden (and later also I. A. Richards) in the 1930s; a recent revival has been initiated by Bill Templer
- Threshold Level English, developed by van Ek and Alexander

- Globish, developed by Jean-Paul Nerrière
- Basic Global English, developed by Joachim Grzega
- Nuclear English, proposed by Randolph Quirk and Gabriele Stein but never fully developed.

Language teaching practice often assumes that most of the difficulties that learners face in the study of English are a consequence of the degree to which their native language differs from English (a contrastive analysis approach). A native speaker of Chinese, for example, may face many more difficulties than a native speaker of German, because German is closely related to English, whereas Chinese is not. This may be true for anyone of any mother tongue (also called first language, normally abbreviated L1) setting out to learn any other language (called a target language, second language or L2).

Language learners often produce errors of syntax and pronunciation thought to result from the influence of their L1, such as mapping its grammatical patterns inappropriately onto the L2, pronouncing certain sounds incorrectly or with difficulty, and confusing items of vocabulary known as false friends. This is known as L1 transfer or "language interference". However, these transfer effects are typically stronger for beginners' language production, and SLA research has highlighted many errors which cannot be attributed to the L1, as they are attested in learners of many language backgrounds (for example, failure to apply 3rd person present singular -s to verbs, as in 'he make').

While English is no more complex than other languages, it has several features which may create difficulties for learners. Conversely, because such a large number of people are studying it, products have been developed to help them do so, such as the monolingual learner's dictionary, which is written with a restricted defining vocabulary.

Pronunciation

- Consonant phonemes

  English does not have more individual consonant sounds than most languages. However, the interdentals, /¸/ and /ð/ (the sounds written with *th*), which are common in English (*thin*, *thing*, etc.; and *the*, *this*, *that*, etc.) are relatively rare in other languages, even others in the Germanic family (*e.g.*, English *thousand* = German *tausend*), and these sounds are missing even in some English dialects. Some learners substitute a [t] or [d] sound, while others shift to [s] or [z], [f] or [v] and even [ts] or [dz]).

  Speakers of Japanese, Korean and Chinese varieties have difficulty distinguishing [r] and [l]. The distinction between [b] and [v] can cause difficulty for native speakers of Spanish, Japanese and Korean.

  Vowel phonemes

  The precise number of distinct vowel sounds depends on the variety of English: for example, Received Pronunciation has twelve monophthongs (single or "pure" vowels), eight diphthongs (double vowels) and two triphthongs (triple vowels); whereas General American has thirteen monophthongs and three diphthongs. Many learners, such as speakers of Spanish, Japanese or Arabic, have fewer vowels, or only pure ones, in their mother tongue and so may have problems both with hearing and with pronouncing these distinctions.

- Syllable structure

  In its syllable structure, English allows for a cluster of up to three consonants before the vowel and four after it (*e.g., straw*, *desks*, *glimpsed*). The syllable structure causes problems for speakers of many other languages. Japanese, for example, broadly alternates consonant and vowel sounds so learners from Japan often try to force vowels in between the consonants (*e.g., desks* /desks/ becomes "desukusu" or *milk shake* /mjlk ʃejk/ becomes "mirukushçku").

  Learners from languages where all words end in vowels sometimes tend to make all English words end in vowels, thus *make* /mejk/ can come out as [mejkY]. The learner's task is further complicated by the fact that native speakers may drop consonants in the more complex blends (*e.g.*, [mŒns] instead of [mŒn¸s] for *months*).

- Unstressed vowels - Native English speakers frequently replace almost any vowel in an unstressed syllable with an unstressed vowel, often schwa. For example, *from* has a distinctly pronounced short 'o' sound when it is stressed (*e.g., Where are you from?*), but when it is unstressed, the short 'o' reduces to a schwa (*e.g., I'm from London.*). In some cases, unstressed vowels may disappear altogether, in words such as chocolate (which has four syllables in Spanish, but only two as pronounced by Americans: "*choc-lit*".)

Stress in English more strongly determines vowel quality than it does in most other world languages (although there are notable exceptions such as Russian). For example, in some varieties the syllables *an*, *en*, *in*, *on* and *un* are pronounced as homophones, that is, exactly alike. Native speakers can usually distinguish *an able*, *enable*, and *unable* because of their position in a sentence, but this is more difficult for inexperienced English speakers. Moreover, learners tend to overpronounce these unstressed vowels, giving their speech an unnatural rhythm.

- Stress timing - English tends to be a stress-timed language - this means that stressed syllables are roughly equidistant in time, no matter how many syllables come in between. Although some other languages, e.g., German and Russian, are also stress-timed, most of the world's other major languages are syllable-timed, with each syllable coming at an equal time after the previous one. Learners from these languages often have a staccato rhythm when speaking English that is disconcerting to a native speaker.

"Stress for emphasis" - students' own languages may not use stress for emphasis as English does.

"Stress for contrast" - stressing the right word or expression. This may not come easily to some nationalities.

"Emphatic apologies" - the normally unstressed auxiliary is stressed (I really *am* very sorry)

In English there are quite a number of words - about fifty - that have two different pronunciations, depending on whether they are stressed. They are "grammatical words": pronouns, prepositions, auxiliary verbs and conjunctions. Most students tend to overuse the strong form, which is pronounced with the written vowel.

Grammar

- Tenses - English has a relatively large number of tenses with some quite subtle differences, such as the difference between the simple past "I ate" and the present perfect "I have eaten." Progressive and perfect progressive forms add complexity. (See English verbs.)
- Functions of auxiliaries - Learners of English tend to find it difficult to manipulate the various ways in which English uses the first auxiliary verb of a tense. These include negation (eg *He hasn't been drinking.*), inversion with the subject to form a question (eg *Has he been drinking?*), short answers (eg *Yes, he has.*) and tag questions (*has he?*). A further complication is that the dummy auxiliary verb *do /does /did* is added to fulfil these functions in the simple present and simple past, but not for the verb *to be*.
- Modal verbs - English also has a significant number of modal auxiliary verbs which each have a number of uses. For example, the opposite of "You must be here at 8" (obligation) is usually "You don't have to be here at 8" (lack of obligation, choice), while "must" in "You must not drink the water" (prohibition) has a different meaning from "must" in "You must not be a native speaker" (deduction). This complexity takes considerable work for most learners to master.
- Idiomatic usage - English is reputed to have a relatively high degree of idiomatic usage. For example, the use of different main verb forms in such apparently parallel constructions as "try to learn", "help learn", and "avoid learning" pose

difficulty for learners. Another example is the idiomatic distinction between "make" and "do": "make a mistake", not "do a mistake"; and "do a favour", not "make a favour".

- Articles - English has an appreciable number of articles , including the definite article *the* and the indefinite article *a, an*. At times English nouns can or indeed must be used without an article; this is called the zero article. Some of the differences between definite, indefinite and zero article are fairly easy to learn, but others are not, particularly since a learner's native language may lack articles or use them in different ways than English does. Although the information conveyed by articles is rarely essential for communication, English uses them frequently (several times in the average sentence), so that they require some effort from the learner.

Vocabulary

- Phrasal verbs - Phrasal verbs in English can cause difficulties for many learners because they have several meanings and different syntactic patterns. There are also a number of phrasal verb differences between American and British English.
- Word derivation - Word derivation in English requires a lot of rote learning. For example, an adjective can be negated by using the prefix *un-* (e.g. *unable*), *in-* (e.g. *inappropriate*), *dis-* (e.g. *dishonest*), or *a-* (e.g. *amoral*), or through the use of one of a myriad of related but rarer prefixes, all modified versions of the first four.
- Size of lexicon - The history of English has resulted in a very large vocabulary, essentially one stream

from Old English and one from the Norman infusion of Latin-derived terms. (Schmitt & Marsden claim that English has one of the largest vocabularies of any known language.) This inevitably requires more work for a learner to master the language.

Differences between Spoken and Written English

As with most languages, written language tends to use a more formal register than spoken language. The acquisition of literacy takes significant effort in English.

- Spelling - Because of the many changes in pronunciation which have occurred since a written standard developed, and the retention of many historical idiosyncrasies in spelling, English spelling is difficult even for native speakers to master. This difficulty is shown in such activities as spelling bees that generally require the memorization of words. English speakers may also rely on computer tools such as spell checkers more than speakers of other languages, as the users of the utility may have forgotten, or never learned, the correct spelling of a word. The generalizations that exist are quite complex and there are many exceptions leading to a considerable amount of rote learning. The spelling system causes problems in both directions - a learner may know a word by sound but not be able to write it correctly (or indeed find it in a dictionary), or they may see a word written but not know how to pronounce it or mislearn the pronunciation.

Varieties of English

- There are thriving communities of English native speakers in countries all over the world, and this historical diaspora has led to some noticeable differences in pronunciation, vocabulary and grammar in different countries, as well as those variations which exist between different regions, and across the social strata, within the same country. Even within the British Isles, there are significant regional language differences, differences of (i) pronunciation/accent, (ii) vocabulary, and even (iii) grammar/dialect, when the local dialect differs from that of another region or from the grammar of 'received English'.

- The world holds over 7000 languages, and most exist within only a small geographic area; even most of the top 100 are limited to a small number of countries or even a single state. Some of the more well-known languages are to some degree managed by a specific organisation that determines the most prestigious form of the language, e.g. French language and the *Academie de la langue française* or Spanish language and the *Real Academia Española*. Since many students of English study it to enable them to communicate internationally, the lack of a uniform international standard for the language poses some barriers to meeting that goal; see international English.
- Teaching English therefore involves not only helping the student to use the form of English most suitable for his purposes, but also exposure to other forms of English (e.g. regional forms/ cultural styles) so that the student will be able to discern 'meaning' even when the words/grammar/pronunciation may be quite different to the form of English with which he has become more familiar.

The Common European Framework

Between 1998 and 2000, the Council of Europe's language policy division developed its Common European Framework of Reference for Languages. The aim of this framework was to have a common system for foreign language testing and certification, to cover all European languages and countries.

The Common European Framework (CEF) divides language learners into three levels:

- A. Basic User
- B. Independent User
- C. Proficient User

Qualifications for Teachers

Non-native Speakers

Most people who teach English are in fact not native speakers of that language. They are state school teachers in countries around the world, and as such they hold the relevant teaching qualification of their country, usually with a specialism in teaching English. For example, teachers in Hong Kong hold the Language Proficiency Assessment for Teachers. Those who work in private language schools may, from commercial pressures, have the same qualifications as native speakers (see below).

United States Qualifications

Most U.S. instructors at community colleges and universities qualify by taking an MA in TESOL. This degree also qualifies them to teach in most EFL contexts as well. In some areas of the country, nearly all elementary school teachers are involved in teaching ELLs (English Language Learners, that is, children who come to school speaking a home language other than English.) The qualifications for these classroom teachers vary from state to state but always include a state-issued teaching certificate for public instruction.

Teachers in all states require state licensing, which requires substantial practical field experiences and language pedagogy course work. The MA in TESOL includes both graduate work in English as one of the classical liberal arts (literature, linguistics, media studies) with a theoretical pedagogical component at the tertiary level.

Admission to the MA in TESOL typically requires at least a bachelor's degree with a minor in English or linguistics. A degree in a foreign language can sometimes also be considered sufficient for admission.

It is important to note that the issuance of a teaching certificate or license is not automatic following completion of degree requirements. All teachers must complete a battery of exams (typically the Praxis subject and method exams or similar, state-sponsored exams) as well as supervised instruction as student teachers.

Certification requirements for ESL teachers vary greatly from state to state. Out-of-state teaching certificates are recognized by other states if the two states have a reciprocity agreement.

British Qualifications

Common, respected qualifications for teachers within the United Kingdom's sphere of influence include TESOL certificates and diplomas issued by University of Cambridge ESOL and Trinity College London ESOL.

A certificate course is usually undertaken before starting to teach. This is sufficient for most EFL jobs (see **TEFL** for an extended discussion of travel-teaching) and for some ESOL ones. CELTA (Certificate in English Language Teaching to Adults) and CertTESOL (Certificate in Teaching English to Speakers of Other Languages) are the most widely taken and accepted qualifications for new teacher trainees.

Courses are offered in the UK and in many countries around the world. It is usually taught full-time over a one-month period or part-time over a period up to a year.

Asian countries now require Certificates based on Asian English Learning (Korean Ministry of Justice -March 2008) whilst China is only acepting (at government school level) certificates authorised by the International Acreditation Authority. Taiwan and Hong Kong are also implementing the certificate coures certified by the independant authority.

Teachers with two or more years of teaching experience who want to stay in the profession and advance their career prospects (including school management and teacher training) can take a diploma course. University of Cambridge ESOL offers the DELTA (Diploma in English Language Teaching to Adults) and Trinity College London ESOL offers the LTCL DipTESOL (Trinity Licentiate Diploma in Teaching English to Speakers of Other Languages). These diplomas are considered to be equivalent and are both accredited at level 7 of the revised National Qualifications Framework.

Some teachers who stay in the profession go on to do an MA in a relevant discipline such as applied linguistics or ELT. Many UK master's degrees require considerable experience in the field before a candidate is accepted onto the course.

The above qualifications are well-respected within the UK EFL sector, including private language schools and higher education language provision. However, in England and Wales, in order to meet the government's criteria for being a qualified teacher of ESOL in the Learning and Skills Sector (i.e. post-compulsory or further education), teachers need to have the Certificate in Further Education Teaching Stage 3 at level 5 (of the revised NQF) and the Certificate for ESOL Subject Specialists at level 4. Recognised qualifications which confer one or both of these include a Postgraduate Certificate in Education (PGCE) in ESOL, the CELTA module 2 and City & Guilds 9488.

Teachers of children within the state sector in the United Kingdom are normally expected to hold a PGCE, and may choose to specialise in ELT.

Types of English

- BE - Business English
- EAL - English as an additional language

The use of this term is restricted to certain countries. See the discussion in Terminology and types.

- EAP - English for academic purposes
- EFL - English as a foreign language

English for use in a non-English-speaking region, by someone whose first language is not English. See the discussion in Terminology and types.

- EIL - English as an international language (see main article at International English)
- ELF - English as a lingua franca
- ELL - English language learner

The use of this term is restricted to certain countries. See the discussion in Terminology and types.

- ELT - English language teaching

  The use of this term is restricted to certain countries. See the discussion in Terminology and types.

- ESL - English as a second language

  English for use in an English-speaking region, by someone whose first language is not English. The use of this term is restricted to certain countries. See the discussion in Terminology and types.

- ESOL - English for speakers of other languages

  This term is used differently in different countries. See the discussion in Terminology and types.

- ESP - English for special purposes, or English for specific purposes (e.g. technical English, scientific English, English for medical professionals, English for waiters).

- TEFL - Teaching English as a foreign language This link is to a page about a subset of TEFL, namely travel-teaching.

More generally, see the discussion in Terminology and types.

- TESL - Teaching English as a second language

  The use of this term is restricted to certain countries. See the discussion in Terminology and types.

- TESOL - Teaching English to speakers of other languages, or Teaching English as a second or other language

- TYLE - Teaching Young Learners English
  - Note that YL Young Learners can mean under 18, or much younger.

3

English Literature

"I had always thought of English literature as the richest in the world; the discovery now of a secret chamber (sc. Old English literature) at the very threshold of that literature came to me as an additional gift." - Jorge Luis Borges, 'An Autobiographical Essay', The Aleph & Other Stories.

English literature is as diverse as the varieties and dialects of English spoken around the world. In academia, the term often labels departments and programmes practising *English studies* in secondary and tertiary educational systems.

This article primarily deals with literature from Britain written in English. For literature from specific English-speaking regions.

Middle Ages

The first works in English, written in Old English, appeared in the early Middle Ages (the oldest surviving text is Cædmon's *Hymn*). The oral tradition was very strong in early British culture and most literary works were written to be performed. Epic poems were thus very popular and many, including *Beowulf*, have survived to the present day in the rich corpus of Anglo-Saxon literature that closely resemble today's Norwegian or, better yet, Icelandic. Much Anglo-Saxon verse in the extant manuscripts is probably a "milder" adaptation of the earlier Viking and German war poems from the continent. When such poetry was brought to England it was still being handed down orally from one generation to another, and the constant presence of alliterative verse, or consonant rhyme (today's newspaper headlines and marketing abundantly use this technique such as in *Big is Better*) helped the Anglo-Saxon peoples remember it. Such rhyme is a feature of Germanic languages and is opposed to vocalic or end-rhyme of Romance languages. But the first written literature dates to the early Christian monasteries founded by St. Augustine of Canterbury and his disciples and it is reasonable to believe that it was somehow adapted to suit to needs of Christian readers. Even without their crudest lines, Viking war poems still smell of blood feuds and their consonant rhymes sound like the smashing of swords under the gloomy northern sky: there is always a sense of imminent danger in the narratives. Sooner or later, all things must come to an end, as Beowulf eventually dies at the hands of the monsters he spends the tale fighting. The feelings of Beowulf that nothing lasts, that youth and joy will turn to death and sorrow entered Christianity and were to dominate the future landscape of English fiction.

England's first great author, Geoffrey Chaucer (1340 - 1400), wrote in Middle English. His most famous work is *The Canterbury Tales*, a collection of stories in a variety of genres, ostensibly told by a group of pilgrims on their way to Canterbury. Remarkably, they are from all walks of life, which is reflected as much in the language they use as in the content of their stories. But, though Chaucer is most certainly an English author, he was inspired by literary developments taking place elsewhere in Europe, especially in Italy. *The Canterbury Tales* are quite indebted to Giovanni Boccaccio's *Decameron*. The Renaissance was making its way to Britain.

Renaissance Literature

Following the introduction of a printing press into England by William Caxton in 1476, vernacular literature flourished. The Reformation inspired the production of vernacular liturgy which led to the Book of Common Prayer, a lasting influence on literary English language. The poetry, drama, and prose produced under both Queen Elizabeth I and King James I constitute what is today labelled as Early modern (or Renaissance).

Early Modern Period

Elizabethan Era

The Elizabethan era saw a great flourishing of literature, especially in the field of drama. The Italian Renaissance had rediscovered the ancient Greek and Roman theatre, and this was instrumental in the development of the new drama, which was then beginning to evolve apart from the old mystery and miracle plays of the Middle Ages. The Italians were particularly inspired by Seneca (a major tragic playwright and philosopher, the tutor of Nero) and Plautus (its comic clichés, especially that of the boasting soldier had a powerful influence on the Renaissance and after).

However, the Italian tragedies embraced a principle contrary to Seneca's ethics: showing blood and violence on the stage. In Seneca's plays such scenes were only acted by the characters. But the English playwrights were intrigued by Italian model: a conspicuous community of Italian actors had settled in London and Giovanni Florio had brought much of the Italian language and culture to England. It is also true that the Elizabethan Era was a very violent age and that the high incidence of political assassinations in Renaissance Italy (embodied by Niccolò Machiavelli's *The Prince*) did little to calm fears of popish plots. As a result, representing that kind of violence on the stage was probably more cathartic for the Elizabethan spectator. Following earlier Elizabethan plays such as *Gorboduc* by Sackville & Norton and *The Spanish Tragedy* by Kyd that was to provide much material for *Hamlet*, William Shakespeare stands out in this period as a poet and playwright as yet unsurpassed. Shakespeare was not a man of letters by profession, and probably had only some grammar school education. He was neither a lawyer, nor an aristocrat as the "university wits" that had monopolised the English stage when he started writing.

But he was very gifted and incredibly versatile, and he surpassed "professionals" as Robert Greene who mocked this "shake-scene" of low origins. Though most dramas met with great success, it is in his later years (marked by the early reign of James I) that he wrote what have been considered his greatest plays: *Hamlet*, *Romeo and Juliet*, *Othello*, *King Lear*, *Macbeth*, *Antony and Cleopatra*, and *The Tempest*, a tragicomedy that inscribes within the main drama a brilliant pageant to the new king. This 'play within a play' takes the form of a masque, an interlude with music and dance colored by the novel special effects of the new indoor theaters. Critics have shown that this masterpiece, which can be considered a dramatic work in its own right, was written for James's court, if not for the monarch himself. The magic arts of Prospero, on which depend the outcome of the plot, hint at the fine relationship between art and nature in poetry. Significantly for those times (the arrival of the first colonists in America), *The*

Tempest is (though not apparently) set on a Bermudan island, as research on the *Bermuda Pamphlets* (1609) has shown, linking Shakespeare to the *Virginia Company itself*. The "News from the New World", as Frank Kermode points out, were already out and Shakespeare's interest in this respect is remarkable. Shakespeare also popularized the English sonnet which made significant changes to Petrarch's model.

The sonnet was introduced into English by Thomas Wyatt in the early 16th century. Poems intended to be set to music as songs, such as by Thomas Campion, became popular as printed literature was disseminated more widely in households. *See English Madrigal School*. Other important figures in Elizabethan theatre include Christopher Marlowe, Thomas Dekker, John Fletcher and Francis Beaumont. Had Marlowe (1564-1593) not been stabbed at twenty-nine in a tavern brawl, says Anthony Burgess, he might have rivalled, if not equalled Shakespeare himself for his poetic gifts. Remarkably, he was born only a few weeks before Shakespeare and must have known him well. Marlowe's subject matter, though, is different: it focuses more on the moral drama of the renaissance man than any other thing. Marlowe was fascinated and terrified by the new frontiers opened by modern science.

Drawing on German lore, he introduced Dr. Faustus to England, a scientist and magician who is obsessed by the thirst of knowledge and the desire to push man's technological power to its limits. He acquires supernatural gifts that even allow him to go back in time and wed Helen of Troy, but at the end of his twenty-four years' covenant with the devil he has to surrender his soul to him. His dark heroes may have something of Marlowe himself, whose untimely death remains a mystery. He was known for being an atheist, leading a lawless life, keeping many mistresses, consorting with ruffians: living the 'high life' of London's underworld. But many suspect that this might have been a cover-up for his activities as a secret agent for Elizabeth I, hinting that the 'accidental stabbing' might have been a premeditated assassination by the enemies of The Crown. Beaumont and Fletcher are less-known, but it is almost sure that they helped Shakespeare write some of his best dramas, and were quite popular at the time. It is also at this time that the city comedy genre develops. In the later 16th century English poetry was characterised by elaboration of language and extensive allusion to classical myths. The most important poets of this era include Edmund Spenser and Sir Philip Sidney. Elizabeth herself, a product of Renaissance humanism, produced occasional poems such as *On Monsieur's Departure*.

Canons of Renaissance Poetry

Jacobean Literature

After Shakespeare's death, the poet and dramatist Ben Jonson was the leading literary figure of the Jacobean era (The reign of James I). However, Jonson's aesthetics hark back to the Middle Ages rather than to the Tudor Era: his characters embody the theory of humors. According to this contemporary medical theory, behavioral differences result from a prevalence of one of the body's four "humors" (blood, phlegm, black bile, and yellow bile) over the other three; these humors correspond with the four elements of the universe: air, water, fire, and earth. This leads Jonson to exemplify such differences to the point of creating types, or clichés.

Jonson is a master of style, and a brilliant satirist. His *Volpone* shows how a group of scammers are fooled by a top con-artist, vice being punished by vice, virtue meting out its reward.

Others who followed Jonson's style include Beaumont and Fletcher, who wrote the brilliant comedy, *The Knight of the Burning Pestle*, a mockery of the rising middle class and especially of those nouveaux riches who pretend to dictate literary taste without knowing much literature at all. In the story, a couple of grocers wrangle with professional actors to have their illiterate son play a leading role in a drama. He becomes a knight-errant wearing, appropriately, a burning pestle on his shield. Seeking to win a princess' heart, the young man is ridiculed much in the way Don Quixote was. One of Beaumont and Fletcher's chief merits was that of realising how feudalism and chivalry had turned into snobbery and make-believe and that new social classes were on the rise. Another popular style of theatre during Jacobean times was the revenge play, popularized by John Webster and Thomas Kyd. George Chapman wrote a couple of subtle revenge tragedies, but must be remembered chiefly on account of his famous translation of Homer, one that had a profound influence on all future English literature, even inspiring John Keats to write one of his best sonnets. The King James Bible, one of the most massive translation projects in the history of English up to this time, was started in 1604 and completed in 1611. It represents the culmination of a tradition of Bible translation into English that began with the work of William Tyndale. It became the standard Bible of the Church of England, and some consider it one of the greatest literary works of all time.

This project was headed by James I himself, who supervised the work of forty-seven scholars. Although many other translations into English have been made, some of which are widely considered more accurate, many aesthetically prefer the King James Bible, whose meter is made to mimic the original Hebrew verse. Besides Shakespeare, whose figure towers over the early 1600s, the major poets of the early 17th century included John Donne and the other Metaphysical poets. Influenced by continental Baroque, and taking as his subject matter both Christian mysticism and eroticism, metaphysical poetry uses unconventional or "unpoetic" figures, such as a compass or a mosquito, to reach surprise effects. For example, in "A Valediction: Forbidding Mourning", one of Donne's Songs and Sonnets, the points of a compass represent two lovers, the woman who is home, waiting, being the center, the farther point being her lover sailing away from her. But the larger the distance, the more the hands of the compass lean to each other: separation makes love grow fonder. The paradox or the oxymoron is a constant in this poetry whose fears and anxieties also speak of a world of spiritual certainties shaken by the modern discoveries of geography and science, one that is no longer the center of the universe. Apart from the metaphysical poetry of Donne, the 17th century is also celebrated for its Baroque poetry. Baroque poetry served the same ends as the art of the period; the Baroque style is lofty, sweeping, epic, and religious. Many of these poets have an overtly Catholic sensibility (namely Richard Crashaw) and wrote poetry for the Catholic counter-Reformation in order to establish a feeling of supremacy and mysticism that would ideally persuade newly emerging Protestant groups back toward Catholicism.

Caroline and Cromwellian Literature

The turbulent years of the mid-17th century, during the reign of Charles I and the subsequent Commonwealth and Protectorate, saw a flourishing of political literature in English. Pamphlets written by sympathisers of every faction in the English civil war ran from vicious personal attacks and polemics, through many forms of propaganda, to high-minded schemes to reform the nation. Of the latter type, *Leviathan* by Thomas Hobbes would prove to be one of the most important works of British political philosophy. Hobbes's writings are some of the few political works from the era which are still regularly published while John Bramhall, who was Hobbes's chief critic, is largely forgotten. The period also saw a flourishing of news books, the precursors to the British newspaper, with journalists such as Henry Muddiman, Marchamont Needham, and John Birkenhead representing the views and activities of the contending parties. The frequent arrests of authors and the suppression of their works, with the consequence of foreign or underground printing, led to the proposal of a licensing system. The *Areopagitica*, a political pamphlet by John Milton, was written in opposition to licensing and is regarded as one of the most eloquent defenses of press freedom ever written.

Specifically in the reign of Charles I (1625 – 42), English Renaissance theatre experienced its concluding efflorescence. The last works of Ben Jonson appeared on stage and in print, along with the final generation of major voices in the drama of the age: John Ford, Philip Massinger, James Shirley, and Richard Brome. With the closure of the theatres at the start of the English Civil War in 1642, drama was suppressed for a generation, to resume only in the altered society of the English Restoration in 1660. Other forms of literature written during this period are usually ascribed political subtexts, or their authors are grouped along political lines.

The cavalier poets, active mainly before the civil war, owed much to the earlier school of metaphysical poets. The forced retirement of royalist officials after the execution of Charles I was a good thing in the case of Izaak Walton, as it gave him time to work on his book *The Compleat Angler*. Published in 1653, the book, ostensibly a guide to fishing, is much more: a meditation on life, leisure, and contentment.

The two most important poets of Oliver Cromwell's England were Andrew Marvell and John Milton, with both producing works praising the new government; such as Marvell's *An Horatian Ode upon Cromwell's Return from Ireland*. Despite their republican beliefs they escaped punishment upon the Restoration of Charles II, after which Milton wrote some of his greatest poetical works (with any possible political message hidden under allegory). Thomas Browne was another writer of the period; a learned man with an extensive library, he wrote prolifically on science, religion, medicine and the esoteric.

Restoration Literature

Restoration literature includes both *Paradise Lost* and the Earl of Rochester's *Sodom,* the high spirited sexual comedy of *The Country Wife* and the moral wisdom of *Pilgrim's Progress*. It saw Locke's *Treatises on Government,* the founding of the Royal Society, the experiments of Robert Boyle and the holy meditations of Boyle, the hysterical attacks on theaters from Jeremy Collier, the pioneering of literary criticism from Dryden, and the first newspapers. The official break in literary culture caused by censorship and radically moralist standards under Cromwell's Puritan regime created a gap in literary tradition, allowing a seemingly fresh start for all forms of literature after the Restoration. During the Interregnum, the royalist forces attached to the court of Charles I went into exile with the twenty-year old Charles II. The nobility who travelled with Charles II were therefore lodged for over a decade in the midst of the continent's literary scene. Charles spent his time attending plays in France, and he developed a taste for Spanish plays. Those nobles living in Holland began to learn about mercantile exchange as well as the tolerant, rationalist prose debates that circulated in that officially tolerant nation.

The largest and most important poetic form of the era was satire. In general, publication of satire was done anonymously. There were great dangers in being associated with a satire.

On the one hand, defamation law was a wide net, and it was difficult for a satirist to avoid prosecution if he were proven to have written a piece that seemed to criticize a noble. On the other hand, wealthy individuals would respond to satire as often as not by having the suspected poet physically attacked by ruffians. John Dryden was set upon for being merely *suspected* of having written the *Satire on Mankind.* A consequence of this anonymity is that a great many poems, some of them of merit, are unpublished and largely unknown.

Prose in the Restoration period is dominated by Christian religious writing, but the Restoration also saw the beginnings of two genres that would dominate later periods: fiction and journalism. Religious writing often strayed into political and economic writing, just as political and economic writing implied or directly addressed religion. The Restoration was also the time when John Locke wrote many of his philosophical works. Locke's empiricism was an attempt at understanding the basis of human understanding itself and thereby devising a proper manner for making sound decisions.

These same scientific methods led Locke to his three

Treatises on Government, which later inspired the thinkers in the American Revolution. As with his work on understanding, Locke moves from the most basic units of society toward the more elaborate, and, like Thomas Hobbes, he emphasizes the plastic nature of the social contract. For an age that had seen absolute monarchy overthrown, democracy attempted, democracy corrupted, and limited monarchy restored, only a flexible basis for government could be satisfying. The Restoration moderated most of the more strident sectarian writing, but radicalism persisted after the Restoration. Puritan authors such as John Milton were forced to retire from public life or adapt, and those Digger, Fifth Monarchist, Leveller, Quaker, and Anabaptist authors who had preached against monarchy and who had participated directly in the regicide of Charles I were partially suppressed. Consequently, violent writings were forced underground, and many of those who had served in the Interregnum attenuated their positions in the Restoration.

John Bunyan stands out beyond other religious authors of the period. Bunyan's *The Pilgrim's Progress* is an allegory of personal salvation and a guide to the Christian life. Instead of any focus on eschatology or divine retribution, Bunyan instead writes about how the individual saint can prevail against the temptations of mind and body that threaten damnation. The book is written in a straightforward narrative and shows influence from both drama and biography, and yet it also shows an awareness of the grand allegorical tradition found in Edmund Spenser. During the Restoration period, the most common manner of getting news would have been a broadsheet publication. A single, large sheet of paper might have a written, usually partisan, account of an event. However, the period saw the beginnings of the first professional and periodical (meaning that the publication was regular) journalism in England. Journalism develops late, generally around the time of William of Orange's claiming the throne in 1689. Coincidentally or by design, England began to have newspapers just when William came to court from Amsterdam, where there were already newspapers being published. It is impossible to satisfactorily date the beginning of the novel in English.

However, long fiction and fictional biographies began to distinguish themselves from other forms in England during the Restoration period. An existing tradition of *Romance* fiction in France and Spain was popular in England. The "Romance" was considered a feminine form, and women were taxed with reading "novels" as a vice. One of the most significant figures in the rise of the novel in the Restoration period is Aphra Behn. She was not only the first professional female novelist, but she may be among the first professional novelists of either sex in England. Behn's most famous novel was *Oroonoko* in 1688. This was a biography of an entirely fictional African king who had been enslaved in Suriname. Behn's novels show the influence of tragedy and her experiences as a dramatist. As soon as the previous Puritan regime's ban on public stage representations was lifted, the drama recreated itself quickly and abundantly. The most famous plays of the early Restoration period are the unsentimental or "hard" comedies of John Dryden, William Wycherley, and George Etherege, which reflect the atmosphere at Court, and celebrate an aristocratic macho lifestyle of unremitting sexual intrigue and conquest. After a sharp drop in both quality and quantity in the 1680s, the mid-90s saw a brief second flowering of the drama, especially comedy. Comedies like William Congreve's *Love For Love* (1695) and *The Way of the World* (1700), and John Vanbrugh's *The Relapse* (1696) and *The Provoked Wife* (1697) were "softer" and more middle-class in ethos, very different from the aristocratic extravaganza twenty years earlier, and aimed at a wider audience.

The playwrights of the 1690s set out to appeal to more socially mixed audiences with a strong middle-class element, and to female spectators, for instance by moving the war between the sexes from the arena of intrigue into that of marriage. The focus in comedy is less on young lovers outwitting the older generation, more on marital relations after the wedding bells. Diarists John Evelyn and Samuel Pepys depicted everyday London life and the cultural scene of the times.

Augustan Literature

The term Augustan literature derives from authors of the 1720s and 1730's themselves, who responded to a term that George I of England preferred for himself. While George I meant the title to reflect his might, they instead saw in it a reflection of Ancient Rome's transition from rough and ready literature to highly political and highly polished literature. Because of the aptness of the metaphor, the period from 1689 - 1750 was called "the Augustan Age" by critics throughout the 18th century (including Voltaire and Oliver Goldsmith). The literature of the period is overtly political and thoroughly aware of critical dictates for literature. It is an age of exuberance and scandal, of enormous energy and inventiveness and outrage, that reflected an era when English, Scottish, and Irish people found themselves in the midst of an expanding economy, lowering barriers to education, and the stirrings of the Industrial Revolution. The most outstanding poet of the age is Alexander Pope, but Pope's excellence is partially in his constant battle with other poets, and his serene, seemingly neo-Classical approach to poetry is in competition with highly idiosyncratic verse and strong competition from such poets as Ambrose Philips.

It was during this time that James Thomson produced his melancholy *The Seasons* and Edward Young wrote *Night Thoughts.* It is also the era that saw a serious competition over the proper model for the pastoral. In criticism, poets struggled with a doctrine of *decorum,* of matching proper words with proper sense and of achieving a diction that matched the gravity of a subject. At the same time, the mock-heroic was at its zenith. Pope's *Rape of the Lock* and *The Dunciad* are still the greatest mock-heroic poems ever written. In prose, the earlier part of the period was overshadowed by the development of the English essay. Joseph Addison and Richard Steele's *The Spectator* established the form of the British periodical essay, inventing the pose of the detached observer of human life who can meditate upon the world without advocating any specific changes in it.

However, this was also the time when the English novel, first emerging in the Restoration, developed into a major artform. Daniel Defoe turned from journalism and writing criminal lives for the press to writing fictional criminal lives with *Roxana* and *Moll Flanders.* He also wrote a fictional treatment of the travels of Alexander Selkirk called *Robinson Crusoe* (1719). The novel would benefit indirectly from a tragedy of the stage, and in mid-century many more authors would begin to write novels. If Addison and Steele overawed one type of prose, then Jonathan Swift did another. Swift's prose style is unmannered and direct, with a clarity that few contemporaries matched. He was a profound skeptic about the modern world, but he was similarly profoundly distrustful of nostalgia.

He saw in history a record of lies and vanity, and he saw in the present a madness of vanity and lies. Core Christian values were essential, but these values had to be muscular and assertive and developed by constant rejection of the games of confidence men and their gullies. Swift's *A Tale of a Tub* announced his skeptical analysis of the claims of the modern world, and his later prose works, such as his war with Patridge the astrologer, and most of all his derision of pride in *Gulliver's Travels* left only the individual in constant fear and humility safe. After his "exile" to Ireland, Swift reluctantly began defending the Irish people from the predations of colonialism. His *A Modest Proposal* and the Drapier Letters provoked riots and arrests, but Swift, who had no love of Irish Roman Catholics, was outraged by the abuses and barbarity he saw around him. Drama in the early part of the period featured the last plays of John Vanbrugh and William Congreve, both of whom carried on the Restoration comedy with some alterations. However, the majority of stagings were of lower farces and much more serious and domestic tragedies.

George Lillo and Richard Steele both produced highly moral forms of tragedy, where the characters and the concerns of the characters were wholly middle class or working class. This reflected a marked change in the audience for plays, as royal patronage was no longer the important part of theatrical success. Additionally, Colley Cibber and John Rich began to battle each other for greater and greater spectacles to present on stage. The figure of Harlequin was introduced, and pantomime theater began to be staged. This "low" comedy was quite popular, and the plays became tertiary to the staging.

Opera also began to be popular in London, and there

was significant literary resistance to this Italian incursion. This trend was broken only by a few attempts at a new type of comedy. Pope and John Arbuthnot and John Gay attempted a play entitled *Three Hours After Marriage* that failed. In 1728, however, John Gay returned to the playhouse with *The Beggar's Opera.* Gay's opera was in English and retold the story of Jack Sheppard and Jonathan Wild. However, it seemed to be an allegory for Robert Walpole and the directors of the South Sea Company, and so Gay's follow up opera was banned without performance. The licensing act of 1737 brought an abrupt halt to much of the period's drama, as the theatres were once again brought under state control. An effect of the Licensing Act was to cause more than one aspiring playwright to switch over to writing novels. Henry Fielding began to write prose satire and novels after his plays could not pass the censors. Henry Brooke also turned to novels.

In the interim, Samuel Richardson had produced a novel intended to counter the deleterious effects of novels in *Pamela, or Virtue Rewarded* (1749). Henry Fielding attacked the absurdity of this novel with two of his own works, *Joseph Andrews* and *Shamela*, and then countered Richardson's *Clarissa* with *Tom Jones*. Brooke wrote *The Man of Feeling* and indirectly began the sentimental novel. Laurence Sterne attempted a Swiftian novel with a unique perspective on the impossibility of biography (the model for most novels up to that point) and understanding with *Tristram Shandy*, even as his detractor Tobias Smollett elevated the picaresque novel with his works.

Each of these novels represents a formal and thematic divergence from the others. Each novelist was in dialogue and competition with the others, and, in a sense, the novel established itself as a diverse and open-formed genre in this explosion of creativity. The most lasting effects of the experimentation would be the psychological realism of Richardson, the bemused narrative voice of Fielding, and the sentimentality of Brooke.

18th Century Literature

During the Age of Sensibility, literature reflected the worldview of the Age of Enlightenment (or Age of Reason) – a rational and scientific approach to religious, social, political, and economic issues that promoted a secular view of the world and a general sense of progress and perfectibility. Led by the philosophers who were inspired by the discoveries of the previous century (Newton) and the writings of Descartes, Locke and Bacon. They sought to discover and to act upon universally valid principles governing humanity, nature, and society. They variously attacked spiritual and scientific authority, dogmatism, intolerance, censorship, and economic and social restraints. They considered the state the proper and rational instrument of progress. The extreme rationalism and skepticism of the age led naturally to deism; the same qualities played a part in bringing the later reaction of romanticism.

Increased emphasis on instinct and feeling, rather than judgment and restraint. A growing sympathy for the Middle Ages during the Age of Sensibility sparked an interest in medieval ballads and folk literature.

Romanticism

The changing landscape of Britain brought about by the steam engine has two major outcomes: the boom of industrialism with the expansion of the city, and the consequent depopulation of the countryside as a result of the enclosures, or privatisation of pastures. Most peasants poured into the city to work in the new factories.

This abrupt change is revealed by the change of meaning in five key words: industry (once meaning "creativity"), democracy (once disparagingly used as "mob rule"), class (from now also used with a social connotation), art (once just meaning "craft"), culture (once only belonging to farming).

But the poor condition of workers, the new class-conflicts and the pollution of the environment causes a reaction to urbanism and industrialisation prompting poets to rediscover the beauty and value of nature. Mother earth is seen as the only source of wisdom, the only solution to the ugliness caused by machines. The superiority of nature and instinct over civilisation had been preached by Jean Jacques Rousseau and his message was picked by almost all European poets.

The first in England were the Lake Poets, a small group of friends including William Wordsworth and Samuel Taylor Coleridge. These early Romantic Poets brought a new emotionalism and introspection, and their emergence is marked by the first romantic Manifesto in English literature, the "Preface to the Lyrical Ballads". This collection was mostly contributed by Wordsworth, although Coleridge must be credited for his long and impressive *Rime of the Ancient Mariner*, a tragic ballad about the survival of one sailor through a series of supernatural events on his voyage through the south seas which involves the slaying of an albatross, the death of the rest of the crew, a visit from Death and his mate, Life-in-Death, and the eventual redemption of the Mariner. Coleridge and Wordsworth, however, understood romanticism in two entirely different ways: while Coleridge sought to make the supernatural "real" (much like sci-fi movies use special effects to make unlikely plots believable), Wordsworth sought to stir the imagination of readers through his down-to-earth characters taken from real life (for eg. in "The Idiot Boy"), or the beauty of the Lake District that largely inspired his production (as in "Lines Composed a Few Miles Above Tintern Abbey").

The "Second generation" of Romantic poets includes Lord Byron, Percy Bysshe Shelley, Mary Shelley and John Keats. Byron, however, was still influenced by 18th-century satirists and was, perhaps the least 'romantic' of the three. His amours with a number of prominent but married ladies was also a way to voice his dissent on the hypocrisy of a high society that was only apparently religious but in fact largely libertine, the same that had derided him for being physically impaired. His first trip to Europe resulted in the first two cantos of Childe Harold's Pilgrimage, a mock-heroic epic of a young man's adventures in Europe but also a sharp satire against London society. Despite *Childe Harold's* success on his return to England, accompanied by the publication of *The Giaour* and *The Corsair* his alleged incestuous affair with his half-sister Augusta Leigh in 1816 actually forced him to leave England for good and seek asylum on the continent. Here he joined Percy Bysshe Shelley, his wife Mary, with his secretary Dr. John Polidori on the shores of Lake Geneva during the 'year without a summer' of 1816. Although his is just a short story, Polidori must be credited for introducing The Vampyre, conceived from the same competition which spawned Mary Shelley's *Frankenstein*, to English literature. Percy, like Mary, had much in common with Byron: he was an aristocrat from a famous and ancient family, had embraced atheism and free-thinking and, like him, was fleeing from scandal in England.

Shelley had been expelled from college for openly

declaring his atheism. He had married a 16-year-old girl, Harriet Westbrook whom he had abandoned soon after for Mary (Harriet took her own life after that). Harriet did not embrace his ideals of free love and anarchism, and was not as educated as to contribute to literary debate. Mary was different: the daughter of philosopher and revolutionary William Godwin, she was intellectually more of an equal, shared some of his ideals and was a feminist like her late mother, Mary Wollstonecraft, author of *Vindication of the Rights of Women*. One of Shelley's best works is the *Ode to the West Wind*. Despite his apparent refusal to believe in God, this poem is considered a homage to pantheism, the recognition of a spiritual presence in nature.

Mary Shelley did not go down in history for her poetry, but for giving birth to science fiction: the plot for the novel is said to have come from a nightmare during stormy nights on Lake Geneva in the company of Percy Shelley, Lord Byron, and John Polidori. Her idea of making a body with human parts stolen from different corpses and then animating it with electricity was perhaps influenced by Alessandro Volta's invention and Luigi Galvani's experiments with dead frogs. Frankenstein's chilling tale also suggests modern organ transplants, tissue regeneration, reminding us of the moral issues raised by today's medicine.

But the creature of Frankenstein is incredibly romantic as well. Although "the monster" is intelligent, good and loving, he is shunned by everyone because of his ugliness and deformity, and the desperation and envy that result from social exclusion turn him against the very man who created him. John Keats did not share Byron's and Shelley's extremely revolutionary ideals, but his cult of pantheism is as important as Shelley's. Keats was in love with the ancient stones of the Parthenon that Lord Elgin had brought to England from Greece, also known as the Elgin Marbles). He celebrates ancient Greece: the beauty of free, youthful love couples here with that of classical art. Keats's great attention to art, especially in his *Ode on a Grecian Urn* is quite new in romanticism, and it will inspire Walter Pater's and then Oscar Wilde's belief in the absolute value of art as independent from aesthetics. The most popular novelist of the era was Sir Walter Scott, whose grand historical romances inspired a generation of painters, composers, and writers throughout Europe.

By contrast, Jane Austen wrote novels about the life of the landed gentry, seen from a woman's point of view, and wryly focused on practical social issues, especially marriage and money. Poet, painter and printmaker William Blake is usually included among the English Romanticists, though his visionary work is much different from that of the others discussed in this section.

Victorian Literature

It was in the Victorian era (1837-1901) that the novel became the leading form of literature in English. Most writers were now more concerned to meet the tastes of a large middle class reading public than to please aristocratic patrons. The best known works of the era include the emotionally powerful works of the Brontë sisters; the satire *Vanity Fair* by William Makepeace Thackeray; the realist novels of George Eliot; and Anthony Trollope's insightful portrayals of the lives of the landowning and professional classes.

Charles Dickens emerged on the literary scene in the 1830s, confirming the trend for serial publication. Dickens wrote vividly about London life and the struggles of the poor, but in a good-humoured fashion which was acceptable to readers of all classes. His early works such as the *Pickwick Papers* are masterpieces of comedy. Later his works became darker, without losing his genius for caricature.

An interest in rural matters and the changing social and economic situation of the countryside may be seen in the novels of Thomas Hardy, Elizabeth Cleghorn Gaskell, and others.

Leading poetic figures included Alfred Tennyson, Robert Browning, Elizabeth Barrett Browning, Matthew Arnold, Dante Gabriel Rossetti, and Christina Rossetti.

Literature for children developed as a separate genre. Some works become globally well-known, such as those of Lewis Carroll and Edward Lear, both of whom used nonsense verse. Adventure novels, such as those of Anthony Hope and Robert Louis Stevenson, were written for adults but are now generally classified as for children.

Modernism

The movement known as English literary modernism grew out of a general sense of disillusionment with Victorian era attitudes of certainty, conservatism, and objective truth. The movement was greatly influenced by the ideas of Romanticism, Karl Marx's political writings, and the psychoanalytic theories of subconscious - Sigmund Freud. The continental art movements of Impressionism, and later Cubism, were also important inspirations for modernist writers.

Although literary modernism reached its peak between the First and Second World Wars, the earliest examples of the movement's attitudes appeared in the mid to late nineteenth century. Gerard Manley Hopkins, A.E. Housman, and the poet and novelist Thomas Hardy represented a few of the major early modernists writing in England during the Victorian period.

The first decades of the twentieth century saw several major works of modernism published, including the seminal short story collection *Dubliners* by James Joyce, Joseph Conrad's *Heart of Darkness*, and the poetry and drama of William Butler Yeats.

Important novelists between the World Wars included Virginia Woolf, E.M. Forster, Evelyn Waugh, P.G. Wodehouse and D.H. Lawrence. T. S. Eliot was the preeminent English poet of the period. Across the Atlantic writers like William Faulkner, Ernest Hemingway, and the poets Wallace Stevens and Robert Frost developed a more American take on the modernist aesthetic in their work.

Perhaps the most contentiously important figure in the development of the modernist movement was the American poet Ezra Pound. Credited with "discovering" both T. S. Eliot and James Joyce, whose stream of consciousness novel *Ulysses* is considered to be one of the century's greatest literary achievements, Pound also advanced the cause of imagism and free verse, forms which would dominate English poetry into the twenty-first century.

Gertrude Stein, an American expat, was also an enormous literary force during this time period, famous for her line "Rose is a rose is a rose is a rose." Other notable writers of this period included H.D., Marianne Moore, Elizabeth Bishop, W. H. Auden, Vladimir Nabokov, William Carlos Williams, Ralph Ellison, Dylan Thomas, R.S. Thomas and Graham Greene. However, some of these writers are more closely associated with what has become known as post-modernism, a term often used to encompass the diverse range of writers who succeeded the modernists.

Post-modern literature

The term Postmodern literature is used to describe certain tendencies in post-World War II literature. It is both a continuation of the experimentation championed by writers of the modernist period (relying heavily, for example, on fragmentation, paradox, questionable narrators, etc.) and a reaction against Enlightenment ideas implicit in Modernist literature. Postmodern literature, like postmodernism as a whole, is difficult to define and there is little agreement on the exact characteristics, scope, and importance of postmodern literature. Henry Miller, William S. Burroughs, Joseph Heller, Kurt Vonnegut, Hunter S. Thompson, Truman Capote, Thomas Pynchon.

4

Indian English Literature

Indian English Literature (IEL) refers to the body of work by writers in India who write in the English language and whose native or co-native language could be one of the numerous languages of India. It is also associated with the works of members of the Indian diaspora, especially people like Salman Rushdie who was born in India. It is frequently referred to as Indo-Anglian literature. (*Indo-Anglian* is a specific term in the sole context of writing that should not be confused with the term *Anglo-Indian*). As a category, this production comes under the broader realm of postcolonial literature- the production from previously colonised countries such as India.

IEL has a relatively recent history, it is only one and a half centuries old. The first book written by an Indian in English was by Sake Dean Mahomet, titled *Travels of Dean Mahomet*; Mahomet's travel narrative was published in 1793 in England. In its early stages it was influenced by the Western art form of the novel. Early Indian writers used English unadulterated by Indian words to convey an experience which was essentially Indian. Raja Rao's *Kanthapura* is Indian in terms of its storytelling qualities. Rabindranath Tagore wrote in Bengali and English and was responsible for the translations of his own work into

English. Dhan Gopal Mukerji was the first Indian author to win a literary award in the United States. Nirad C. Chaudhuri, a writer of non-fiction, is best known for his *The Autobiography of an Unknown Indian* where he relates his life experiences and influences. P. Lal, a poet, translator, publisher and essayist, founded a press in the 1950s for Indian English writing, Writers Workshop.

R.K. Narayan is a writer who contributed over many decades and who continued to write till his death recently. He was discovered by Graham Greene in the sense that the latter helped him find a publisher in England. Graham Greene and Narayan remained close friends till the end. Similar to Thomas Hardy's Wessex, Narayan created the fictitious town of Malgudi where he set his novels. Some criticise Narayan for the parochial, detached and closed world that he created in the face of the changing conditions in India at the times in which the stories are set. Others, such as Graham Greene, however, feel that through Malgudi they could vividly understand the Indian experience. Narayan's evocation of small town life and its experiences through the eyes of the endearing child protagonist Swaminathan in *Swami and Friends* is a good sample of his writing style. Simultaneous with Narayan's pastoral idylls, a very different writer, Mulk Raj Anand, was similarly gaining recognition for his writing set in rural India; but his stories were harsher, and engaged, sometimes brutally, with divisions of caste, class and religion.

Later History

Among the later writers, the most notable is Salman Rushdie, born in India, now living in the United Kingdom. Rushdie with his famous work *Midnight's Children* (Booker Prize 1981, Booker of Bookers 1992) ushered in a new trend of writing. He used a hybrid language – English generously peppered with Indian terms – to convey a theme that could be seen as representing the vast canvas of India. He is usually categorised under the magic realism mode of writing most famously associated with Gabriel García Márquez.

Bharati Mukherjee, author of *Jasmine* (1989), has spent much of her career exploring issues involving immigration and identity with a particular focus upon the United States and Canada.

Vikram Seth, author of *A Suitable Boy* (1994) is a writer who uses a purer English and more realistic themes. Being a self-confessed fan of Jane Austen, his attention is on the story, its details and its twists and turns.

Shashi Tharoor, in his *The Great Indian Novel* (1989), follows a story-telling (though in a satirical) mode as in the Mahabharata drawing his ideas by going back and forth in time. His work as UN official living outside India has given him a vantage point that helps construct an objective Indianness.

Other authors include Anita Desai, Kiran Desai, Arundhati Roy, Chitra Banerjee Divakaruni, Raj Kamal Jha, Jhumpa Lahiri, Bharti Kirchner, Khushwant Singh, Amit Chaudhuri, Amitav Ghosh, Vikas Swarup, Rohinton Mistry, Kiran Nagarkar and C R Krishnan.

Debates

It would be useful at this point to bring in the recent debates on Indian Writing in English ("IWE").

One of the key issues raised in this context is the superiority/inferiority of IWE as opposed to the literary production in the various languages of India. Key polar concepts bandied in this context are superficial/authentic, imitative/creative, shallow/deep, critical/uncritical, elitist/ parochial and so on.

The views of Rushdie and Amit Chaudhuri expressed through their books *The Vintage Book of Indian Writing* and *The Picador Book of Modern Indian Literature* respectively essentialise this battle.

Rushdie's statement in his book – "the ironic proposition that India's best writing since independence may have been done in the language of the departed imperialists is simply too much for some folks to bear" – created a lot of resentment among many writers, including writers in English. In his book, Amit Chaudhuri questions – "Can it be true that Indian writing, that endlessly rich, complex and problematic entity, is to be represented by a handful of writers who write in English, who live in England or America and whom one might have met at a party?"

Chaudhuri feels that after Rushdie, IWE started employing magical realism, bagginess, non-linear narrative and hybrid language to sustain themes seen as microcosms of India and supposedly reflecting Indian conditions. He contrasts this with the works of earlier writers such as Narayan where the use of English is pure, but the deciphering of meaning needs cultural familiarity. He also feels that Indianness is a theme constructed only in IWE and does not articulate itself in the vernacular literatures. (It is probable that the level of Indianness constructed is directly proportional to the distance between the writer and India.) He further adds "the post-colonial novel, becomes a trope for an ideal hybridity by which the West celebrates not so much Indianness, whatever that infinitely complex thing is, but its own historical quest, its reinterpretation of itself".

Some of these arguments form an integral part of what is called postcolonial theory. The very categorisation of IWE – as IWE or under post-colonial literature – is seen by some as limiting. Amitav Ghosh made his views on this very clear by refusing to accept the Eurasian Commonwealth Writers Prize for his book *The Glass Palace* in 2001 and withdrawing it from the subsequent stage.

The renowned writer V.S. Naipaul, a third generation Indian from Trinidad and Tobago and a Nobel prize laureate, is a person who belongs to the world and usually not classified under IWE. Naipaul evokes ideas of homeland, rootlessness and his own personal feelings towards India in many of his books.

Jhumpa Lahiri, a Pulitzer prize winner from the U.S., is a writer uncomfortable under the label of IWE.

Recent writers in India such as Arundhati Roy and David Davidar show a direction towards contextuality and rootedness in their works. Arundhati Roy, a trained architect and the 1997 Booker prize winner for her *The God of Small Things*, calls herself a "home grown" writer. Her award winning book is set in the immensely physical landscape of Kerala. Davidar sets his *The House of Blue Mangoes* in Southern Tamil Nadu. In both the books, geography and politics are integral to the narrative. In his novel Lament of Mohini (2000), Shreekumar Varma touches upon the unique matriarchal system and the *sammandham* system of marriage as he writes about the Namboodiris and the aristocrats of Kerala.

As the number of Indian writers in English keeps increasing, with everyone with a story to tell trying to tell a story, and as publishing houses in India vie among themselves to discover the next new whiz-kid who will land up with world fame, it could become increasingly difficult to separate the wheat from the chaff. Research, debates and seminars on IWE continue with increasing frequency. However,it might be too early a stage in the history of Indian writing in English to pass any final judgement.

Poetry

A much over-looked category of Indian writing in English is poetry. As stated above, Rabindranath Tagore wrote in Bengali and English and was responsible for the translations of his own work into English. Other early notable poets in English include Derozio, Michael Madhusudan Dutt, Joseph Furtado, Armando Menezes, Toru Dutt, Romesh Chandra Dutt, Sarojini Naidu and her brother Harendranath Chattopadhyaya.

In modern times, Indian poetry in English was typified by two very different poets. Dom Moraes, winner of the Hawthornden Prize at the precocious age of 19 for his first book of poems "A Beginning" went on to occupy a pre-eminent position among Indian poets writing in English. Nissim Ezekiel, who came from India's tiny Bene Israel Jewish community, created a voice and place for Indian poets writing in English and championed their work.

Their contemporaries in English poetry in India were Arvind Mehrotra, Jayanta Mahapatra, Gieve Patel, A.K. Ramanujan, Rajagopal Parthasarathy, Keki Daruwala, Adil Jussawala, Arun Kolatkar, Dilip Chitre, Eunice De Souza, Kersi Katrak, P. Lal and Kamala Das among several others.

A generation of exiles also sprang from the Indian diaspora. Among these are names like Agha Shahid Ali, Sujata Bhatt, Melanie Silgardo and Vikram Seth.

The current generation of Indian poets writing in English includes Ranjit Hoskote, Smita Agarwal, Gopi Kottoor, Jeet Thayil, Tishani Doshi, Tabish Khair, Vijay Nambisan, H. Masud Taj, Rukmini Bhaya Nair, C.P. Surendran,Imtiaz Dharker, Vivek Narayanan, Samartha Vashishtha, Meena Kandasamy, Gavin Barrett, Anjum Hasan, Jerry Pinto, Shreekumar Varma, Arundhathi Subramaniam, Anand Thakore, Meena Alexander, Gayatri Majumdar, A.J. Thomas, Kumar Vikram ,Thachom Poyil Rajeevan and Mohit K. Misra.

Indo-Nostalgic Writing

Indo-Nostalgic writing is a somewhat loosely defined term encompassing writings, in the English language, wherein nostalgia regarding the Indian subcontinent, typically regarding India, represent a dominant theme or strong undercurrent. The writings may be memoirs, or quasi-fictionalized memoirs, travelogues, or inspired in part by real-life experiences and in part by the writer's imagination. This would include both mass-distributed "Indo-Anglian" literature put out by major publishing houses and also much shorter articles (e.g. feature pieces in mainstream or literary magazines) or poetry, including material published initially or solely in webzines.

Certainly, Indo-Nostalgic writings have much overlap with post-colonial literature but are generally not about 'heavy' topics such as cultural identity, conflicted identities, multilingualism or rootlessness. The writings are often less self-conscious and more light-hearted, perhaps dealing with impressionistic memories of places, people, cuisines,

Only-in-India situations, or simply vignettes of "the way things were".

Of late, a few Indo-nostalgic writers are beginning to show signs of "long-distance nationalism", concomitant with the rise of nationalism within India against the backdrop of a booming economy. In addition to focusing on nationalism or any universal themes, many writers emerged out with innovative ideas and techniques in writing poetry. It is a pity that there are many writers whose writings still remain unnoticed either due to lack of source to get their works recoganised or less opportunities does not knock the doors of the right person.

Writers like Krishna Srinivas, M.K.Gopinathan, etc have contributed enormous poetry collection to the growth of Indian English Literature. Krishna Srinivas concentrated on all sorts of social aspects in his poetry, and M.K.Gopinathan poetic mission is to spread peace in the minds of the readers. M.K.Gopinathan's anthologies includes, "I go on for ever", "A Fresh Rose" and "It is not my fault" which contained interesting subjects of day to day life. Typically, the authors are either Western-based writers of Indian origin (e.g. Salman Rushdie, Rohinton Mistry), or Western writers who have spent long periods of time in the subcontinent, possibly having been born or raised in India, perhaps as the children of British Raj-era European expatriates or missionaries (e.g. Jim Corbett, Stephen Alter).

Or, they may even be Anglo-Indians who have emigrated from the subcontinent to the West. Third Culture Kids (TCKs) often grow up to produce Indo-Nostalgic writings that exhibit palpably deep (and perhaps somewhat romanticized) feelings for their childhoods in the subcontinent. Accordingly, another common theme in Indo-

Nostalgic writing is "rediscovery" or its cousin, "reconnection".

No doubt, for mass-distributed authors, Indo-Nostalgic writings may not necessarily represent *all* of their literary output, but certainly would represent a high percentage; it is their sweet spot, after all.

5

Research in Bilingual Proficiency Development

The research studies reviewed here use a variety of methodological and analytical procedures to focus on the development of bilingual proficiency under different social and educational conditions. The initial chapters focused on the cognitive and linguistic consequences of different pattern bilingual proficiency. This research suggested that access to two languages in early childhood can promote children's metalinguistic awareness and possible also broader aspects of cognitive development. The conclusion that positive metalinguistic and cognitive consequences can result from the interaction between L1 and L2 is consistent with the notion of a 'common underlying proficiency' that emerges from the findings of bilingual education programmes for minority and majority language children.

The interdependence of L1 and L2 development is further supported by studies of age and L2 acquisition and by investigations of bilingual language use at home. These studies also allowed us to conclude that a distinction must be made between using language in a richly contextualized situation and using language where cues to meaning come primarily from the test itself. For young second language learners who are surrounded by native-speaking children of the target language, peer-appropriate levels of context-embedded L2 skills and attained more rapidly than is the case for academically-related aspects of proficiency. The frequent misuses of standardized tests with minority students and common misconceptions regarding the consequences of bilingual education can be traced to a failure to take account of the distinction between context-embedded and context-reduced language skills and the fact that academic skills in L1 and L2 are manifestations of the same underlying dimension. A somewhat different perspective on these issues is provided by the research that focuses on the components of communicative competence. Several studies have used factor analytic methods to investigate the validity of various proposed components of communicative competence.

Bachman and Palmer (1982), for example, examined the extent to which grammatical, sociolinguistic and pragmatic competence (discourse competence in the Canale and Swain [(1980a) framework, subsequently elaborated in Canale (1983)] were separate traits. Although fairly clear conceptual distinctions can be made between these three components, studies using confirmatory factor analysis have produced what appear to be equivocal findings. Bachman and Palmer (1982), for example, were unable to distinguish grammatical and pragmatic competence in their study involving university level ESL students.

Our own confirmatory factor analyses with grade 6 French immersion students appeared to produce little evidence for the proposed distinctions. It has been assumed by many researchers that the way to assess the structure of language proficiency is to use factor analytic methods.

Obviously the emergence of discrete factors would constitute evidence for the validity of distinguishing specific dimensions. On the other hand, it became clear to us as we worked with our data that failure of the hypothesized factors to emerge did not preclude the possibility of their being distinguishable using other analytical techniques or in other groups of learners with different language learning experiences.

This is because factor analysis does not take into account the determinants of proficiency (as does, for example, regression analysis). Thus, the central empirical focus for future factor analytical studies should move from an attempt to test *absolute* models of communicative competence to an attempt to predict and test which components of communicative competence will become differentiated from each other for particular groups of language learners in specific acquisition contexts. Furthermore, if in a factor analysis, predicted factors do not emerge, this does not mean that other analytical methods might not reveal distinct components. Indeed, further analyses of the grade 6 French immersion data suggested that the factor analytic procedures were providing a somewhat restricted perspective on the nature of second language proficiency. In particular, comparisons with native French speakers showed that differences between immersion and native French-speaking students wee minimal on those discourse and sociolinguistic indices where grammatical knowledge plays an insignificant role in achieving correct performance.

Differences between native speakers and immersion students, however, were highly significant on most grammatical measures and on those discourse and sociolinguistic measures where grammatical knowledge was essential for the production of correct linguistic forms.

Additionally, it has been found that early immersion students approach native-speaker levels of proficiency in French reading and listening measures by the end of elementary school but significant differences remain with respect to oral and written grammatical skills. What seems to emerge from this is a distinction between grammatical competence, on the one hand, and sociolinguistic and discourse competence, on the other.

Specifically, grammatical competence (and aspects of sociolinguistic and discourse competence that depend on grammatical knowledge) is acquired in different ways and determined by different factors than is the case with most aspects of discourse and socio-linguistic competence.

These findings raise the issue of what it is about discourse and sociolinguistic competence (abstracted from grammatical competence) that permits L2 learners in a French immersion programme to achieve close to native-speaker proficiency while grammatical competence remains far from native-like.

It is in considering what it is that permits immersion students to achieve native-speaker proficiency in non-grammatical aspects of discourse and sociolinguistic competence but not in grammatical competence that the two strands of research begin to come together and point towards a theoretical synthesis.

Two questions are useful in synthesizing the research data: first, within context-embedded and context-reduced modes, to what extent is the development of grammatical, discourse, and sociolinguistic proficiency a function of exposure to the L2? Second, within context-embedded and context reduced modes, to what extent are L2 grammatical, discourse and sociolinguistic proficiency related to cognitive or personal attributes of the individual? Based on the data from both majority and minority situations that we have reviewed, the answers that we propose to these questions are as follows: first, in both context-embedded and context-reduced modes, the development of L2 grammatical proficiency is more dependent on exposure to L2 than is the development of L2 discourse and sociolinguistic proficiency. Second, within the context-embedded mode, the development of *grammatical* proficiency is not significantly related either to cognitive attributes of the individual or to L1 grammatical proficiency; within the context-reduced mode, on the other hand, cognitive and personal attributes of the individual play a significant determining role in the development of discourse, sociolinguistic and grammatical proficiency.

The Japanese minorities student data reported in Chapter 5 provide a means of testing this hypothesis. First, it can be noted that variables concerned with morphology and syntax loaded on one factor which was distinct from the factors on which the cohesion measure loaded. Secondly, of all the variables derived from the interview with students in their second language, only the index of cohesion in describing a sequence of pictures loaded above .5 on the academic factor. Thirdly, indices of students' background and personal attributes were more strongly related to both English academic proficiency and measures of interactional style than they were to grammatical proficiency.

The converse was true for indices of students' exposure to and use of English which related strongly to grammatical proficiency but much less to academic proficiency and interactional style. Examination of the determinants of academic proficiency and interactional style showed that cognitive variables accounted for the former relationships while personality variables accounted for the latter. In another study involving grade 7 Portuguese background students in Toronto, we have also been examining the nature and determinants of different aspects of bilingual proficiency. We assessed students' grammatical, discourse and sociolinguistic competencies in both English and Portuguese and in both oral and written modalities. Three subgroups of students were assessed: one received oral grammar, discourse and sociolinguistic tests and written discourse tests in each language; the other two received either written sociolinguistic or grammar tests in each language.

Of the written measures, only the written sociolinguistic test involved productive use of the language while the grammar and discourse tests involved multiple choice responses. A complete description of the measures is provided in Cummins, Harley and Swain.

Our analyses revealed that grammatical proficiency in the oral (context-embedded) mode was unrelated across languages but there was evidence of some cross-lingual relationship for both oral discourse and sociolinguistic proficiency. In the written (context-reduced) mode, strong cross-lingual relationships were observed for grammatical, discourse and sociolinguistic proficiencies. Students' oral grammatical competence in Portuguese (their L1 but weaker language) was more strongly related to exposure to and opportunities to use the language than was the case for discourse and sociolinguistic competence. These results are consistent with other research. Saville-Troike (1984), for example, studies a group of ESL learners to determine what second language learning variables best predicted academic achievement. She found that measure of L2 morphology and syntax did not correlate with academic achievement (as measured by the reading subtest of the CTBS), a finding in keeping with our results. She also found that although there was a low correlation between school achievement and time spent using English in interaction with peers or adults, there was a positive and significance correlation between learners' time spent using English and measures of their grammatical knowledge.

Her findings suggest, as do our results, that grammatical proficiency is more dependent on exposure to and use of the L2 than is L2 academic proficiency. Saville-Troike concludes her study by noting that 'we need to recognize that there is a qualitative difference between the communicative tactics and skills that children find effective for meeting their social needs and goals and those that are necessary for successful *academic* achievement in the classroom' (1984, p. 216). Thus, what emerges from these studies is support for the hypothesis that context-embedded grammatical L2 skills develop primarily as a function of exposure to and use of the L2 in the environment whereas L2 academic skills are relatively more dependent on cognitive attributes of the individual. The fact that French immersion students tend not to develop native-like patterns of French grammatical skills in either written or oral modalities can be accounted for by their limited opportunity to interact with native French speakers. The native-like proficiency attained by immersion students in reading and discourse skills can be explained by the fact that the development of these skills is determined by cognitive attributes of the individual, at least as much as they are by exposure to and use of the language in the environment. Why do immigrant students attain proficient L2 grammatical skills within a relatively short time whereas French immersion students continue to experience difficulty in these areas? The same hypotheses appears relevant to this phenomenon.

Immigrant students tend to gain peer-appropriate grammatical skills, at least in the oral modality, considerably more rapidly than is the case of immersion students precisely because their contact with use of the L2 is far greater. The relatively greater influence of cognitive as compared to exposure/use variables on L2 academic skills development is consistent with the fact that for both immigrant and immersion groups, acquisition of age-appropriate L2 academic skills tends to take about the same time, roughly between five and seven years of exposure to L2. The distinction between two broad types of L2 proficiency, namely, attribute-based and input-based proficiency allows the interdependence hypothesis to be placed into a broader framework insofar as all attribute-based aspects of proficiency will be interdependent across languages.

This would not be the case for input-based aspects of proficiency. The model of attribute-based proficiency suggested by the present findings proposes that, for example, L1 and L2 interactional style (in the Japanese student data) are interdependent as a result of the fact that both are, to a significant extent, manifestations of personality attributes of the individual. Similarly, L1 and L2 cognitive/ academic proficiency are interdependent as a result of the fact that both are, to a significant extent, manifestations of the same underlying cognitive proficiency.

A synthesis of the two theoretical perspectives which oriented the data collection and analyses of studies reported in several chapters of this book has thus been suggested from the research evidence. In brief, L2 grammatical proficiency in both context-embedded and context-reduced by the individual. Development of context-reduced L2 grammatical proficiency also depends significantly on attributes of the individual whereas this is not the case, to the same extent, for L2 context-embedded grammatical proficiency.

Discourse and sociolinguistic proficiency, on the other hand, appear less dependent on exposure to the L2 in the environment and, in the context-reduced mode, are attribute-based in that strong cross-lingual and cognitive relationships are observed. Just as we might expect these relationships and the structure of language proficiency to vary according to learner attributes and the nature of the learning environment, so we might expect them to vary with the stage of acquisition. for example, if grammar is taught in the initial stages of L2 learning, then a relationship between cognitive attributes and context-embedded grammatical competence might emerge and grammatical and discourse competence might not show up as separate components of proficiency.

Our hypothesis would be, however, that it would be L2 exposure/use variables that would primarily predict context-embedded grammatical proficiency in the long run. By the same token, L2 exposure/use variables may be strongly related to discourse proficiency in the early stages of second language learning, but cognitive variables, we would predict, would primarily explain the long-term individual differences. In this concluding chapter we have attempted to sketch directions towards which a theory of L2 communicative proficiency might be oriented. A considerable amount of research is required, however, in order to fill in the specifics of such a theory. It is insufficient merely to examine relationships between hypothesized components of proficiency in just one language learning situation, for one group of learners who are at a particular stage of proficiency and cognitive development. Rather, specific hypotheses must be generated regarding the interactions between different components of proficiency (e.g. grammatical, discourse and sociolinguistic in both context-embedded and context-reduced modes) for learners at different developmental levels (e.g. adults, adolescents, young children) from different cultural and linguistic backgrounds (e.g. Chinese L1 compared to Portuguese L1), who are experiencing different patterns both of L2 exposure in the environmental and formal teaching at school. Additionally, it is necessary to take account of the likelihood that very different relations may be observed in the early stages of acquisition than at later stages.

II

LANGUAGE EXPERIENCE AND TEXT

First, it is important that educational problems related to the literacy skills of linguistic minority children have generated much research in the area of sociocultural influences on learning, particularly the contextual and interactional factors in inferring meaning from text.

Researchers concerned with text comprehension have moved ethnographic approaches into the forefront of literacy research (Au and Jordan, 1981; Au and Kawakami, 1984; Diaz, Moll and Mehan, 1986; Erickson, 1984; Gilmore, 1983; Heath, 1983; Moll and Diaz, 1987; Scheffelin and Cochran-Smith, 1984; Scollon and Scollon, 1984; Tannen, 1982; Tharp and Gallimore, 1988; Trueba, 1984).

Central to this research is the meaning of literacy acquisition as a phenomenon taking place in specific social and cultural environments by means of social interaction

(Tharp and Gallimore, in press). Social interactions provide the principal vehicle by which learning and development occur. Children's cognitive skills develop according to the level and amount of interaction with adults or peers in learning environments of which classroom literacy activities are a part.

According to Tharp and Gallimore (1988), children's learning is measured by the distance between their ability to perform a task independently and the level attained with the assistance of more knowledgeable others. This constitutes Vygotsky's (1978) notion of the zone of proximal development which requires teacher involvement in order to provide children with the appropriate practice to move them through their respective zone, a perspective also advanced by Diaz, Moll and Mehan (1986), Moll and Diaz (1987), Tharp and Gallimore (1988), Erickson (1982), Scribner and Cole (1981), and Wertsch (1985).

Children internalise what they learn from the adult or peer and are then able to perform independently in their problem-solving tasks. Text-related content and the means to deal with it are thus learned through socially constructed behavior in which the teacher, each student and peers, have definite roles (Cook-Gumperz, 1986; Erickson, 1984). This study supports the theoretical premise that the learning is socially constructed through meaningful interaction. Teacher interaction with the Spanish-speaking novice readers in this third-grade classroom shows how Spanish-speaking students respond to the teacher's instructional strategies in their effort to comprehend their reading text.

In this study, 'novice' refers to students who are beginning readers, and does not necessarily imply 'low' ability. It is the researcher's contention that students exhibit high or low reading performance not as a result of static traits of fixed intelligence; rather they perform according to the level of expectations and the level and quality of teacher interaction in a socially constituted activity. The teacher, however, has labeled the novice readers as 'low' readers in contrast with high readers who, according to the teacher, are 'better' readers.

Classroom literacy activities provided the primary unit of analysis and thus an explanation for the term 'literacy is required. This term is useless unless we clarify its significance to the people who use it. In this study, the focus is on text comprehension in relation to the children's sociocultural experience of literacy and the way children appear competent in the social context in which their reading ability is evaluated. This definition emerged as the study progressed and the categories were identified.

Three major questions guided the research: (1) How are daily classroom reading lessons organised in the novice reading group? (2) What conditions constrain or enhance student participation in the reading lesson? (3) What conditions change novice students' performance in literacy activities?

Mrs. Cota's third grade class in Marina School was selected as the research site. In this bilingual class, the students were placed in high and low Spanish-speaking reading groups. On the first day of school, Mrs. Cota assessed all of her students according to their reading ability in order to place them in a group with other students of similar ability. Students remained in those same groups through the school year. The advanced reading groups scored at a mean of 79% on the Spanish Comprehensive Tests of Basic Skills, while the mean score for the low readers was 30% and those students relegated to the low reading groups read at least one full year below their respective grade level. Of particular concern to Mrs. Cota were the Spanish-speaking novice readers. Mrs. Cota believed that the seven Spanish speaking students in the novice reading group did not comprehend the text they read. She also believed that they were behind in reading since they had not yet learned to read well in Spanish and they still had to transition to English reading.

The teacher's behavior toward the novice group conformed with her belief that these students had to be treated 'very strictly' because that was the best way for them to 'catch-up' with the skills of advanced readers.

Method

The principal unit of analysis was the classroom reading lesson. Over a three month period, observations of the low-reading group were conducted three times during their reading lesson. Fieldnotes, audio and video recording were used to collect data. Teacher and student interviews were also collected.

Following the micro-ethnographic observations and interviews, an intervention was designed to implement a literacy activity based on the premise of the 'Experience-Test-Relationship' (ETR), reading lesson, an alternative structure for learning to comprehend text. The ETR literacy technique designed in the Kamehameha Early Education Program (KEEP) (Au, 1979) provided a context in which Hawaiian students who were traditionally low in reading skills could utilised their native experience as a basis for discussing the reading text stories. The intervention in reading was initially implemented by me; later I trained the teacher to conduct the experimental lesson based on the ETR approach.

Methodologically, the concept of intervening in the

setting as part of ethnographic data collection has been discussed by Trueba (1979) and Moll and Diaz (1987) as an ethnographic pedagogy Essentially, ethnographic research leads to specific experimental practices such as the introduction of the ETR method which in turn redirect ethnographic inquiry by clarifying areas for additional data collection.

The classroom literacy activity data will be discussed in two major categories, the structure and organisation of the reading lesson and the content interaction between the teacher and the students.

The Daily Reading Lesson

The teacher typically used the 'round robin reading circle' for reading instruction. Mrs. Cota called the students to sit around the table for reading in their textbooks and written tasks in their workbooks Reading lessons were conducted in Spanish because students were limited English speakers. The teacher stood facing the students to tell them that they would be talking about the 'point of the story'. Before the story was discussed, the teacher flashed cards with the new words to the students and called on different students individually to read a word.

Following this initial exercise, the teacher asked the students to read and answer two specific questions which related to the point of the story. The students read individually and silently. The teacher allowed a twenty-minute period for the students to read the assigned number of pages. Before the teacher even began to ask questions, the students often raised their hands to volunteer an answer as if they were going to ask a question. The teacher usually ignored the hands; sometimes she reminded the students that no questions had been asked and to please lower their hands. The teacher then posed questions about the reading.

The following example is one lesson presented by Mrs. Cota to the novice group. It illustrates that the students may not have understood the question posed by the teacher. When called upon to respond, students called out an answer, attempting to demonstrate knowledge. The teacher, however, viewed their answers as incorrect and considered them as evidence of a comprehension problem.

Text 1

[Seven students sat in their reading group. The teacher spent the first fifteen minutes of the lesson drilling the students on new vocabulary words to be found in the story. First she flashed each word to the entire group and told them to repeat it after her. New words included, *cerca* 'near', *montana* 'mountain', and *encontro* 'came across'. After several rounds of repeating the words as a group, the teacher flashed a card to each student around the table and they repeated the word. Then, she asked each student to go up to the board; she dictated each word and they wrote it. If they misspelled it, she asked the group to help them spell it correctly. As instructed by the teacher, the students began to read their story abut the coyote and the mountain. The teacher then asked questions about the fable they had read.]

T: *¿Por donde andaba el coyote tan simpatico que era pero tan s-o-s-p-e-c-h-o-s-o?*

(Said the teacher in a low, deep voice and she squinted her eyes to convey suspicion.)

(Where was the coyote wandering? He was so charming but so s-u-s-p-i-c-i-o-u-s.)

[All hands wave enthusiastically, and T. calls on student B.]

B: *¿Por la montana?*

(By the mountain?)

T: *Pues cerca de la montana. ¿Verdad? ¿Y, que hacia el Coyote ese dia?*

[Well near the mountain. Right? And what was the coyote doing on that day?)

[All hands wave enthusiastically, and T. calls on S.]

S: *¿Buscando comida?*

(Looking for food?)

T: *Si, y ¿que se encontro?*

(Yes, and what did she find?)

[All hands wave enthusiastically, and T. calls on students G.]

Group: *¿Un lobo?*

(A wolf?)

T: *No, no es lobo. ¿Es, que? ¿Que es?*

(No, it's not a wolf. It's a what, what is it?)

G: *!Yo se, yo se, yo se!*

(I know, I know, I know!)

T: *Mario.*

M: *Es una zorra.*

(It's a fox.)

T: *Si una zorra. ¿Y que queria hacer la zorra?*

(Yes, it's a fox and what did the fox want to do?)

[All hands wave anxiously, and T. calls on G.]

G: *Queria comer.*

(It wanted to eat.)

T: *No, ¿Quien sabe?*

(No. Who knows?)

[All hands wave anxiously, and T. calls on H.]

H: *No queria dejarse del coyote?*

(It didn't want to gibe in to the coyote?)

T: *No, A ver, ¿queien se acuerda?*

(No, let's see who remembers?)

[All hands wave anxiously, and T. calls on M. Another student, B. puts his hand down and opens his book to a page and reads it silently while the others are anxiously trying to answer a question.]

M: *¿Queria comerse al coyote?*

(It wanted to eat the coyote?)

T: *No, ustedes no estan pensando. Piensen en que queria hacer la zorra antes de encontrarse con el coyote.*

(No, you're not thinking. Think about what the fox was doing before he ran into the coyote.)

Group: [All hands go up anxiously.) *!Yo se, yo se, yo se!*

(I know, I know, I know!)

[And the teacher calls on student B, who meanwhile has been leafing through his book looking for the section to which the T. referred in her question.]

B: *La zorra iba caminando cerca de la montana pensando como iba a conseguir el ramo de uvas que veia en los altos de la montana.*

(The fox was walking near the mountain thinking about how he was going to get a bunch of grapes that was hanging from the mountain.)

T: *Exacto. Muy bien eso iba pensando la zorra.*

(Exactly. Very good, that's what the fox was thinking.)

[The teacher spent about half an hour on this part of the discussion which represented the first one-forth of the fable. She then stopped and told the students that they would continue on the following day. She assigned workbook exercises in which the students to match a word in the story with the correct meaning.]

Mrs. Cota's questions to the students emphasised surface structure, not meaning. The teacher initially allowed for turn taking so that most of the students were getting a chance to respond to one of her questions. The pattern changed when she noticed that the students did not remember exactly what the fox wanted to do before meeting up with the coyote. She began looking for a student who she thought might have a correct response. When the teacher asked *¿Quien sabe?* 'Who knows?' the students recognised that the teacher was searching for a specific point and their hands waved enthusiastically.

At the point the students were prepared to answer the teacher's question with any fact that they recalled about the story. The students' behavior showed that their goal was the need to please the teacher not to comprehend text. This explains why the students' statements were framed as questions, expressing uncertainty that their answers matched the questions. Student B realised that he could find the answer in the book. Thus, while the teacher searched for someone to answer, he re-read the section that answered the question, displaying appropriate strategic behavior. He did not rely on his memory to guess at the answer. Nevertheless, the teacher either missed or ignored that part where student B re-read the section in the story. The teacher's questions were based on recall only, not inference, which did not encourage interaction among the students or between the teacher and the students. Her questions largely ignored the students' previous knowledge (Au and Kawakami, 1984). The teacher concerned herself with the students getting all parts of the story correct. She believed that the most effective way of testing comprehension meant asking direct 'right and wrong' questions which all students were expected to answer easily.

The teacher's goal of getting precise answers to her questions actually interfered with her clarification questions. For example, she asked *¿Que queria hacer la zorra?* 'What did the fox want to do?' She then rejected two answers by G. and H. which were correct, according to the story, but did not refer to the exact place in the story that she had in mind. Furthermore, she failed to clarify exactly what part of the story she was referring to until M. said, *¿Queria comerse al coyote?* 'It wanted to eat the coyote?' It occurred to her that the students might be guessing, and it was then that she re-framed her question and gave them more clues about where the fox was before meeting up with the coyote. One of the important things to notice is that the group spent an inordinate amount of time constructing these small details of only one-fourth of the fable without any discussion as to the meaning of these facts.

Text 1 shows that this teacher equated comprehension with memorisation and memorisation with learning. She concentrated on getting the students to recall the storyline in sequence. She assumed that children had to be drilled on vocabulary words before they could understand the text and that comprehension comprised a list of facts linked together. Her assumptions reflect the notion of one correct meaning of text, not various socially constructed meanings largely based on sociocultural experience which children bring into the reading lesson. Her emphasis on memorisation created difficulties. Some students memorise better than others. Possibly what we see here is that those students who do not memorise as quickly learn differently, but the fact that they may not memorise as quickly as others does not qualify them as slow learners. It should be noted that despite the insistence on a single route to comprehension, the teacher's interaction style conveyed a sincere and pleasant attitude toward the children. The students responded well to her strict but kind manner. She teased during the lesson by exaggerating a character. Clearly she was interested in helping the students learn.

Phase 1: Redefining Comprehension

Hawaiian children's low comprehension and reading achievement demanded reorganisation of reading lessons in the KEEP classrooms (Au, 1979; Au and Jordan, 1981). The major innovation stressed the importance of learning comprehension by building linkages between the students' experience and new information in the text (Brown *et al.*, 1983; Calfee *el al.*, 1981; Flavell *et al.*, 1981; Griffin and Cole, 1984). The traditional lesson presented by Mrs. Cota had three phases, a drill on vocabulary, an introduction to the reading, and a discussion about the story.

The KEEP lessons fundamentally increased the role of discussion before and after reading. KEEP referred to the lesson as a three-fold model, Experience, Text, and Relationship (ETR).

Elements of the KEEP ETR program include:

(a) the cultural compatibility through the use of the Hawaiian 'talk story' discourse;

(b) the use of previous experience as a basis for understanding text: and

(c) teacher/student questioning strategies at interaction

based on the Vygotskian notion of assisted performance.

These comprehension strategies have enhanced the reading performance of Hawaiian students (Au and Kawakami, 1984; Calfee *et al.*, 1981; Tharp and Gallimore, 1988). This model became the basis for the ethnographic pedagogy which I carried out in this third grade class with Spanish-speaking students.

After intensive observation of Mrs. Cota's third-grade literacy lessons, it became apparent that the novice Spanish-speaking students needed a great deal of special attention. Mrs. Cota asked me if I could work with these students to help them during the school day. I constructed a plan for developing comprehension based on the analysis of the observational data and the ETR model by working with each student individually. This took the form of a pedagogy designed to examine the problem of comprehension as perceived by the teacher. The sessions alternated in two different formats. In one format, the students read a story which they had not read previously from their assigned book. In the second one, they read from a book of their choice.

In each case the procedure was as follows. The students were asked if they had previous knowledge about the subject. In most cases, they did. This led to an open discussion between the researcher and the student with the child taking the lead in the discussion. I assisted them in organising the content into a sequence they understood. They answered questions about their own version of the story pertaining to 'characters', 'sequence of events', 'analysis', 'interpretation', 'feelings', 'opinions', and 'predictions'. In answer to the question, 'what was the most important part of this story to you?' the students consistently shared a part of emotional significance to them.

For example, one student's personal story was about his mischievous dog in Mexico and a series of comical events involving his dog. By describing these events, the student lessened the hurt he felt at leaving his dog, a treasured companion, behind in Mexico. During the literacy activity, the pace was usually fast and lively as the students regaled me with their stories. Following these questions, the students were asked to read the story either in the text or library book; they were reminded that this was also a story like the one they had just told me about a similar topic. They read it silently and were asked to request assistance on any words they did not know or on any part they did not understand. Students frequently asked for help on words but not on comprehending any part of the story. After reading the story, they re-told it in their own words.

Most of the time the students were able to relate the story in proper order with the correct characters as they appeared in the text. Using the students' cues, I proceeded to ask more analytical questions about the story and related it to the characters. For example, questions were asked that made the students look at how one character related to another or how one part of the story related to another, i.e. 'What part of the story was funniest to you?'

The students made comparisons and contrasts and expressed freely their opinions and beliefs about the stories they read. Except for some more analytical questions such as, 'How would another pet like a cat behave differently than your dog?' little prompting or probing was ever necessary in this part of the session. In more advanced sessions, toward the end of the school year, I asked the students to write their personal stories instead of telling them to me orally. I reviewed their stories with them in a formal similar to their oral stories. This process required longer periods of time and often required more than one session. The students began to understand that their written stories were just like those in the books. Fore example, one student commented, *Yo se este fin del cuento em mi libro — Es como el cuento que escribi aqui.* (He pointed to his journal). 'I know where the ending is in the story in my book. It's like the one in the story I wrote'.

This helped them to demystify the stories in the textbook and to begin seeing how it was possible for them to put their own words in some form that made sense. The students were expected to form complete sentences as much as possible such that when they re-read their own story it would read smoothly. The students included words from the text that they found difficult even though these words were never listed as potential new items in the text. The words that the students found difficult were often not the same ones that the textbook writers envisioned and included in the 'new vocabulary word list' in the story.

To sum up, the experience phase included four principal elements:

(1) It introduced meaning to the students' reading through exploring their own experience.

(2) Students reconstructed the structure of a textbook story after they learned how to reconstructed their own story verbally. Through appropriate prompts from the researcher, this relationship could be characterised by a triangle showing connections between the student, a more competent other and the text.

(3) As they had done for their personal stories, students answered analytical questions about the textbook stories and determined their overall meanings.

(4) Students discussed formal relationships between experience and the text to amplify understanding of text-related features of the story such as characters, storyline, and meaning of story.

Reconfiguring the Reading Group

Group reading comprehension lessons were devised by the researcher based on three factors found to be significant in the individual sessions with the students.

These features included:

(a) maximising teacher/student interaction;

(b) utilising students' personal experience to reconstruct the sequence of text; and

(c) generating comparative relationships between text and personal experience to construct high level analytical questions.

The approach varied somewhat from the Experience Text Relationship (ETR) process conducted by Au and Kawakami (1984). That is, I did not move the students from their experience to the text and then draw relationships between the two. Rather, I first listened to the students' experiences; then we discussed the relationship to the text; and then, they read the text. This approach had, however, the Vygotskian theoretical perspective in common.

The following is a example of a group reading lesson within the framework of the ethnographic pedagogy.

[Seven children sat and listened to the story read orally by the researcher. The story dealt with animals that performed in the circus and a special type of animal found by a little boy, who trained an ant to dance.]

R: *¿Que es un circo?*
(What's a circus?)

S1: *¿A donde va uno a ver animales?*
(Where one goes to see animals?)

T: *¿Quienes de ustedes han ido al circo?*
(Who has been to the circus?)

Group: *!Yo fui!Yo fui!*
(I went! I went!)

T: *Si, pues parece que algunos de ustedes han ido [al circo] y otros todavia no tienen esa oportunidad pero ojala una vez pueden ir. Los que no han ido al circo personalmente, pueden saber mucho del circo porque a la mejor conocen a alguien que fue al circo o han visto un circo en libros o la television.*
(Yes, well it looks like some of you have been [to the circus] and others have not yet had that that opportunity but hopefully you'll be able to do so. The ones who have not been to the circus personally, you may know a great deal about the circus because you may know someone who has been to a circus or maybe you've seen one in books or on television.

S2: *Si, yo vi un circo grandote en un cine.*
(Yes I saw a big circus in a movie.)

T: *¿Cuales animales se encuentran?*
(Which animals do you find?)

S2: *Son grandes.*
(They're big.)

S3: *Hay elefantes y changos, y caballos y muchos otros.*

(There are elephants and monkeys and horses and lots of others.)

T: *¿Que piensan los demas sobre lo que dice S3? ¿Cuales otros animales se encuentran en el circo? Me gustaria que tambien se hablaran uno con otro. Por ejemplo, S2 puede dirijir sus comentarios a S3 no solo tienen que dirijirse a mi.*

(What do the rest of you think about what S3 said? Which animals do you find in the circus? I would like you to talk to each other too. For example, S2 can ask questions or make comments directly to S3 not just to me.)

S4: [Looked at the teacher then at looked at S3]

Yo creo que hay otros animales en el circo como una vez yo vi unos leones y tigres.

(I think that there are other animals in the circus like one time I saw some lions and tigers.)

[The lesson continued until the researcher had discussed what roles the circus animals performed and what the boy in the story found in the circus that was different from what was typically found there.]

The lesson exemplified here began with a group activity that posed a question which the group collectively had to negotiate and discuss. The researcher's question forced them to think about a personal experience. 'Have you ever been to the circus? Some of you have and others have not'. The message was that if you had not been to the circus, there were other ways to know about it. It was then possible to participate in the discussion because they had many sources of knowledge.

Following a brief a discussion among the students,

they shared their findings and were then told to read their story silently. The task was to find out what unusual animal the boy in the story had found in the circus. The students were also reminded that they could assist each other with unfamiliar words and with any parts that were difficult for them. The students were left along to read with each other for a while. When the students were through with the short story, the focus of the discussion was determined by the students' interest. The researcher provided a sequence of questions to the students which were framed according to their previous comments. An effort was made to have the students use the facts they recalled about the text to arrive at a higher level analysis about the text.

The following is an account of a part of the literacy event.

Text 2

CD: *¿Se sorprendieron por algo que paso en el cuento?*
(Were you surprised by any part of the story?)

S1: *!Yo se!Yo se!*
(I know! I know!)

S2: *Las hormigas.*
(The ants.)

S3: *Brincaban y bailaban. Que curiosas.*
(They jumped and danced, how cute.)

S4: *Y habia osos tambien, grandotes.*
(And there were bears too, big ones.)

CD: *¿Y por que es raro ver a hormiguitas en un circo?*
(Why is it strange to see ants in a circus?)
[Pause for a few seconds and then the hands went up.]

S3: *¿por que son chiquitas?*

(Because they are small.)

CD: *¿Por que es tan raro que las hormiguitas chiquitas bailen?*

(Why is it so strange that the small ants dance?)

S1: *Por que bailaban y casi nunca se ven hormiguitas bailando.*

(Because you never see ants dancing.)

CD: *Entonces, ¿como es que habia hormiguitas en este circo?*

(Then how did the ants get in the circus?)

S2: *Yo se, es que a unos ninos los llevaron alli y les ensenaron a bailar.*

(I know the children took them there and taught them to dance.)

CD: *¿Creen ustedes que es possible ensenar a las hormiguitas bailar?*

(Do you think it's possible to teach ants to dance?)

[The students continued to interact with the adult and with each other. With the exception of two factual question, the rest were more open ended interpretive level questions.]

The attempt was to focus less on isolated facts of the story and to make the students interact with each other and the teacher at a level that allowed them to use the interactive context, their cultural knowledge, and their interpretive skills to comprehend text. The questions illustrated a responsive teaching approach based on a conversational exchange that built on the students' proceeding utterances.

Transformation of Reading Comprehension Lesson

Four major points of contrast emerged between the ethnographic pedagogy process and the instructional observations of the teacher completed prior to the training on the ethnographic pedagogy procedure:

(1) In the traditional literacy event, the teacher interacted with one individual student at a time. In contrast, the variation of the Experience—Text-Relationship approach provided a context in which all student encouraged to participate not only with teachers but also with peers. It encouraged students to listen to each other because discussion was based. on students' comments.

(2) The intent of the questions about the text also differed. In the traditional approach, the teacher generally tested for recall while the scaffolding approach to inquiry had as its purpose a comprehension process that combined existing knowledge with new knowledge from text to achieve a synthesis.

(3) The types of question differed in that the traditional approach to comprehension often limited the level of questions to memorisations, whereas the scaffolding approach relied on comments generated by use of advance cognitive organisers to respond to questions about the text.

(4) The use of literacy tools (listening, reading, writing) in the traditional approach is restricted primarily to individualised reading with minimal writing done often only in workbooks. The sociocultural literacy process integrated listening, reading and writing for the purpose of understanding the synthesis between previous and new knowledge.

Discussion about the students' experience as it related to their assigned text affected their knowledge acquisition level. The students relegated to a 'low' reading group were only low from the standpoint that they had not been taught how to read meaningfully. The ethnographic pedagogy transformed the inequity in the instructional practices to opportunities in the structional process in two specific ways. First, students became meaningfully engaged in literacy activities when there was a relationship made between their personal knowledge and the written text. This suggests that these students learn experientially. Second, the organisation of interaction provided the students the opportunity to interact meaningfully with the teacher and peers. This occurred when the teacher tailored the questions to the students' comments and built on the level of difficulty which accommodated their cognitive development.

This interactive context demonstrated that learning occurred in social interaction with others who were knowledgeable and can mediated the process. Scholars hold that literacy is best learned when such interaction relates to real life (Tharp and Gallimore, 1988; Vygotsky, 1978; Wertsch, 1985). In order for children to make sense of text, they must be provided with the opportunity to use their sociocultural experience to interact with the text, as they were in the interventions described here.

Summing Up

The process of acquiring literacy and sociocultural knowledge are intimately related. When the teacher isolated the text from the student's experience, the lesson created a skewed representation of the student's ability. In this study, students demonstrated increased comprehension when the social setting was varied and reorganised.

Their comprehension was enhanced when the interactive context in which they were engaged built new knowledge from previous experience. This study illustrated a pedagogical approach based on an interactive theory of reading comprehension. Its primary claim is that both the ability to comprehend text and the very content of literacy are learned through socially constructed behavior, not through rehearsal of facts isolated from the reader's own experience. This claim implies that educators need to look beyond conveniently packaged reading programs that reduce reading to simplistic, mechanistic decoding techniques and consider how children's experiences relate to their literacy acquisition.

Additional research is crucial in the area of literacy and Spanish-speaking Mexican students. This study uncovered the need to look beyond just the language issues in teaching literacy. Educators must begin to maximise literacy acquisition through changing patterns of teacher/student interaction as well as interaction between peers. Micro-ethnographic methods combined with a design for more adaptive pedagogy can provide a vehicle to understand how children learn reading comprehension.

REFERENCES

Au, K.H. and Kawakami, A. (1984) Vygotskian perspective on discussion process in small-group reading lessons. In P.L. Peterson, L.C. Wilkinson and M. Hallinan (eds.) *The Social Context of Instruction: Group Organisation and Group Process* (pp. 209-25). New York: Academic Press.

Briggs, P. and Underwood, G. (1982) Phonological coding in good and poor readers. *Journal of Experimental Child Psychology* 34. 93-112.

Brown, A.L., Bransford, J.D., Ferrara, R.A. and Campione, J.C. (1983) Learning remembering and understanding. In J.H.

Flavell and E.M. Markman (eds) *Handbook of Child Psychology Vol. 3, Cognitive Development* (4th edn) (pp. 77-166). New York: Wiley and sons.

Calfee R.C., Cazden, C.B. Duran, R.P., Griffin M., Martus, M. and Willis, H.D. (1981) Designing reading instructions for cultural minorities: The case of the Kamehameha Early Education Program. Report on the KEEP program. Honolulu, HI.

Carpenter, P.A. and Just, M.A. (1986) Cognitive process in reading. In *Reading Comprehension from Research to Practice* (pp. 11-30). Hillsdale, NJ: Lawrence Erlbaum Associates.

Cook-Gumperz, J. (1986) *The Social Construction of Literacy*. Cambridge: Cambridge University Press.

Delgado-Gaitan, C. (in press) Adult literacy: New directions for Mexican immigrants. In S. Goldman and H.T. Trueba (eds.) *Becoming Literate in English as a Second Language: Advances in Research and Theory*. Norwood, NJ: Ablex.

Diaz, E. Moll, L. and Mehan, H. (1986) Socio-cultural resources in instruction: A context-specific approach. In California State Department Bilingual Education Office (ed.) *Beyond Language: Social and Cultural Factors in Schooling Language Minority Students* (pp. 187-230). Los Angeles, CA: Evaluation, Dissemination and Assessment Center.

Erickson, F. (1984) School literacy, reasoning, and civility: An anthropologist's perspective. *Review of Educational Research* 54, 525-46.

Gilmore, P. (1983) Spelling Mississippi: Recontextualising a literacy related speech event. *Anthropology and Education Quarterly* 14, 235-55.

Griffin, P. and Cole, M. (1984) Current activity for the future: The zo-ped. In B. Rogoff and J. Wertsch (eds) *Children's Learning in Zone of Proximal Development* (pp. 45-64). San Francisco, CA: Jossey-Bass, Inc.

Heath, S.B. (1983) *Ways With Words*. Cambridge: Cambridge University Press.

Moll, L. and Diaz, S. (1987) Change as a goal of educational research. *Anthropology and Education Quarterly* 18, 300-11

Schieffelin, B. and Cochran-Smith, C. (1984) Learning to read culturally: Literacy before schooling. In H. Goelman, A. Oberg and F. Smith (eds) *Awakening to Literacy* (pp. 3-23). London: Heinemann Educational Books.

Scollon, R. and Scollon, S. (1984) 'Looking it up and boiling it down!' Abstracts in Athbaskan children's story retellings. In D. Tannen. (ed.) *Coherence in Spoken and Written Discourse* (pp. 173-95). Norwood, NJ: Ablex.

Tannen, D. (ed.) (1982) *Spoken and Written Language.* Norwood, NJ: Ablex.

Tharp, G.R. and Gallimore, R. (1988) *Rousing Minds to Life: Teaching, Learning, and Schooling in Social Context.* Cambridge, MA: Cambridge University Press.

Trueba, H.T. (1979) Ethnographic research in bilingual education. *Proceedings of the Workshop on Language Policy* (pp. 65-69). University of Illinois, Division of Applied Linguistics.

Vygotsky, L.S. (1978) *Mind in Society,* Cambridge, MA: Harvard University Press.

Weisner, T. and Gallimore, R. (1985) The convergence of ecocultural and activity theory. Paper read at the annual meetings of the American Psychological Association, Washington, DC, December, 1985.

6

Various Linguistic Issues

Many linguistic issues have arisen in relation to the spelling of the words *euro* and *cent* in the many languages of the member states of the European Union, as well as in relation to grammar and the formation of plurals. The official ruling is quite strict, stating "*Community law requires a single spelling of the word "euro" in the nominative singular case in all Community and national legislative provisions, taking into account the existence of different alphabets.*", as well as "*the name of the single currency (euro) is spelled identically in all language versions*". Furthermore, all current and future member states of the eurozone are legally obliged to "observe these principles and guidelines" and to "take such measures as may be necessary to ensure their implementation"

Consequently, the spelling as it appears on the banknotes, is *EURO* in the Latin script and *ÅÕÑÙ* in the Greek script. The Cyrillic spelling *ÅÂÐÎ* will most likely first appear on the banknotes in 2010.

Like the name "euro", the form "cent" is officially required in all member countries to be used in legislation in both the singular and in the plural, e.g. "The currency will be denominated in euro and cent".

The exception is Greece, which uses *ëåðôü* (leptü, Singular), *ëåðôÜ* (leptá, Plural) on the national face of its coins. Immutable word formations have been encouraged by the European Commission in usage with official EU legislation (originally in order to ensure uniform presentation on the banknotes), but the "unofficial" practice concerning the mutability (or not) of the words differs between the member states and their languages. The subject has led to debate and controversy.

However, the Directorate-General for Translation, the EU's translation service, recommends that in English language texts the regular plurals 'euros' and 'cents' should be used in non-legal documents *intended for the general public*.

Bulgarian

Bulgarian uses the Cyrillic alphabet. The current design of euro banknotes has the word *euro* written in both the Latin and Greek alphabets, and it is reasonable to expect that design will be modified to add a Cyrillic inscription. The same is true of euro coins, but if the Greek model is followed, the alternative spelling will go on the national (obverse) side. In popular Bulgarian usage the currency is referred to as åâðî /È[v.ro/; (from Bulgarian Åâðîïà /[v.'ro.pa/ , meaning *Europe*) the plural varies in spoken language – åâðî, åâðà /[v.Èra/, åâðîòà /È[v.ro.ta/ – but the most widespread form is åâðî – without inflection in plural. The word for euro, though, has a normal form with the postpositive definite article – åâðîòî (the euro).

The word for eurocent is åâðîöåíò /È[v.ro.¦[nt/ and most probably that, or only öåíò /¦[nt/, will be used in future when the European currency is accepted in Bulgaria. In contrast to euro, the word for "cent" has a full inflection both in the definite and the plural form: åâðîöåíò (basic form), åâðîöåíòúò (full definite article – postpositive), åâðîöåíòîâå (plural), 2 åâðîöåíòà (numerative form – after numerals). The word stotinki (ñòîòèíêè), singular stotinka (ñòîòèíêà), the name of the subunit of the current Bulgarian currency can be used in place of cent, as it has become a synomym of the word "coins" in colloqiual Bulgarian; just like "cent" (from latin centum), its etymology is from a word meaning hundred - "sto"(ñòî). Stotinki is used widely in the Bulgarian diaspora in Europe to refer to subunits of currencies other than the Bulgarian lev

Initially, the ECB and the EU Commission insisted that Bulgaria change the name it uses for the currency from ÅÂÐÎ to ÅÓÐÎ, claiming the currency should have an official and standard spelling across the EU. Bulgaria on the other hand stated that it wants to take into account the different alphabet and the principle of phonetic orthography in the Bulgarian language.

The issue was decisively resolved in favour of Bulgaria at the 2007 EU Summit in Lisbon, allowing Bulgaria to use the Cyrillic spelling åâðî on all official EU documents.

As of 13 December 2007, all EU institutions - including the ECB - use ÅÂÐÎ as the official Bulgarian transliteration of the single European currency.

Catalan

In Catalan, the official plural is the same as its regular plural "euros". In Eastern Catalan, despite the fact that its regular and official pronunciation is *euro* /È[u.~u/, *euros* /È[u.~us/ many people pronounce it /Èeu.~o/, /Èeu.~os/ as in Spanish. For the cent, the word "cèntim" (plural "cèntims") is used. The fraction of the peseta was also called *cèntim*, but it was withdrawn from circulation decades ago.

Croatian

The spelling *euro* is used in Croatia.

Czech

In Czech, the words *euro* and *cent* are spelt the same as in English and pronounced per Czech phonology /[Š.~T/ , /¦[nt/. Occasionally the word *eurocent* is used instead of *cent* to distinguish the euro denomination versus its foreign counterparts. The spelling differs from the Czech word for Europe (*Evropa*); however "euro-" has become a standard prefix for all things relating to EU (*Evropská unie*). Sometimes German-like pronunciation /Tj~T/ appears jokingly.

The Czech declension uses the different form of plural for various numerals: for 2, 3 and 4 (and rarely 21, 22, 23, 24, 31 etc.) it is plain nominative *eura* and *centy*, while for numbers above 5 genitive (a vestige of partitive) *eur* and *centù*. For *euro*, these grammatically correct declensions are often ignored and non-declinated *euro* is used for every value.

In Czech *euro* is of neuter gender and inflected as *mìsto*, while *cent* is masculine and inflected as *hrad*.

Danish

The word *euro* is included in the 2002 version of Retskrivningsordbogen, which is the authoritative source for the Danish language (according to Danish law). Two plurals are given, *euro* when used about an amount, and *euroer* when used about coins. Both *cent* and *eurocent* are mentioned, the plural and singular forms are identical.

Dutch

Plural: In Dutch, most abstract units of measurement

are not pluralised, causing an amount such as 5 *Euro* to be pronounced as 5 *Euro*, as was previously the case with the Dutch gulden and the Belgian franc. This coincides with EU legislation stating that *euro* and *cent* should be used as both singular and plural. In Dutch, the words are however pluralised as *euro's* and *centen* when referring to individual coins or in other non-abstract cases.

Like the euro, the gulden was divided into 100 *cent*. The Belgian franc was divided into 100 *centiemen*.

Pronunciation: The word *euro* is pronounced in different ways. Most commonly, it's pronounced as /roĐ/, /Đ/ being the standard way to pronounce the eu digraph before an r in Dutch (and the same sound as the /eu/ in *Europa* ("Europe")). Alternatively, some people say /œyroĐ/, using a pronunciation of the /eu/ common in Dutch words of Greek origin, as in *euthanasie* ("euthanasia").

Slang terms: In the Netherlands, slang terms that were previously applied to guilder coinage and banknotes are applied to euro currency. Examples in the Netherlands include *stuiver* for 5 cents, *dubbeltje* for 10 cents.

In Belgium, some Flemings refer to the 1, 2 and 5 cent coins as *koper*, which is the Dutch word for copper, the metal these coins are made of (compare nickel); in the Netherlands it is often called "kopergeld" – 'copper money'. Another nickname is *ros* which means redhead, referring to the colour of the coins.

Syntax: In the Dutch language, the euro sign is chiefly placed before the amount, from which it is often separated by a (thin) space. This was also the case with the florin sign (*f*).

English

Official practice followed in English-language EU legislation is to use the words *euro* and *cent* as both singular and plural. This practice originally arose out of legislation intended to ensure that the banknotes were uncluttered with a string of plurals. Because the *s*-less plurals had become "enshrined" in EU legislation, the Commission decided to retain those plurals in English in legislation even while allowing regular plurals in other languages. The Directorate-General for Translation recommends that in all material intended for the general public, the regular plurals, *euros* and *cents*, be used. The European Commission Directorate-General for Translation's *English Style Guide* (A handbook for authors and translators in the European Commission) states: *"Like 'pound', 'dollar' or any other currency name in English, the word 'euro' is written in lower case with no initial capital and, where appropriate, takes the plural 's' (as does 'cent'): This book costs ten euros and fifty cents."*

In Ireland

As the euro was being adopted in Ireland the Department of Finance decided to use the word *euro* as both the singular and plural forms of the currency, and because Irish broadcasters took their cue from the Department, the "legislative plurals" tend to also be used on the news and in much Irish advertising. This has had the effect of reinforcing the *s*-less plurals, although advertisements made in the UK for broadcast in Ireland tend to use the plurals *euros* and *cents*.

While many in Ireland use the "legislative" plurals *euro* and *cent*, it is also the case that many people in Ireland continue to use the regular plurals *euros* and *cents*. (No census is likely to be made of the relative percentages.)

At the time the *s*-less plurals were introduced, at least some people complained that the EU ought not attempt to "change English grammar". (This was a misunderstanding of the "legislative plural" policy. The Commission has made it clear that local conventions for plural formation should apply in most contexts and the "legislative plural" is expected only in a narrow range of contexts—that is, only in legislation. On the other hand, it remains the case that Irish broadcasters are not following the Commission's recommendations.) People who have become accustomed to what they hear on daily television and radio use the *s*-less plurals. These are also seen written on the notes and coins, though this is less likely to influence usage than broadcasting.

Any number of rationales were subsequently applied to explain why the *s*-less plural might be acceptable, but these are generally folk etymologies. Long-standing plurals in *-s* for currencies that have singular forms ending in *-o*, like pesos and escudos, are relevant when considering the plural of the euro currency. (Compare also the plural of the name of the marsupials known as the Euro.) While it is true that *s*-less plurals exist in English for some other currencies (such as the yen, won, rand and baht), this usage is not the *reason* that the *s*-less plural for the euro was introduced

Usage of both the legislative and regular plurals is widespread in Ireland.

In Australia, Canada, UK, and the USA

Common usage in the rest of the English-speaking world is to use the regular plurals. The media in the UK prefer *euros* and *cents* as the plural forms. Broadcasts of currency exchange rates outside of the European Union tend to use the plural in *-s*, with NPR in the United States and CBC in Canada being two examples. The British comedy television series *The Mighty Boosh* is set in the UK but money is always said to be in "euros".

The term euro-cent is sometimes used in countries (such as Australia, Canada, and the United States which also have "cent" as a currency subdivision), to distinguish them from their local coin. This usage, though unofficial, is perhaps understandable since the coins themselves have the words "EURO" and "CENT" displayed on the common side. The terms "eurodollar", which commonly refers to U.S. dollar deposits outside the United States, or "euro dollar" which is the spoken form of the EUR/USD currency pair in the foreign exchange markets, have occasionally been used, confusingly, to refer to the euro in other parts of the world, particularly non-EU countries such as Australia, Canada, and the United States.

Slang Terms

In Ireland, the slang term *quid* has been transferred from the Irish pound to the euro, with widespread usage. The terms *fiver* and *tenner* (originally for 5 pound- and 10 pound-notes respectively) have carried over as reference to euro notes, and *grand* for a thousand of any currency is also commonly used. In the younger population the terms 'yo(s)' and 'yoyo(s)' are also said to be in common usage.

Finnish

The Finnish pronunciation for "euro" is [Èeu.ro]. In Finnish, the form *sentti* is used for the cent — 'c' is not used in Finnish, and nativized Finnish words cannot end in consonants like '-nt', therefore a vowel 'i' is added. Finnish does not have irregular declinations, so *euro* and *sentti* are regular and decline accordingly. With numerals, the partitive singulars *euroa* and *senttiä* are used, e.g., *10 euro*. This is abbreviated *10 euro*, where the *euro* symbol takes the role of the word *euroa*. The colon notation must not be used with the partitive of *euro* when the number is in nominative. In general, colon notation should be avoided.

Plurals (e.g. *kymmenet eurot* "tens of euros") exist, but they are not used with singular numbers (e.g. *kymmenen euroa* "ten euro").

Sentti is problematic in that its primary meaning is "centimeter". Thus, the officially recommended abbreviation of *sentti* is *snt*, although Finnish merchants generally use a decimal notation (for example *0.35 euro*).

Slang terms: In Helsinki slang, a slang word for euro is *ege*.

French

In French the official plural is the same as the regular plural *euros*. The Académie Française, which is regarded as an authority for the French language in France, stated this clearly, following French legislation in this regard.

The term *cent/cents* [s[nt]/[s[nt] is official in France and Belgium, but is in competition (mainly in France) with *centime/centimes* (the French name for one one-hundredth of the former French or Belgian franc), in part to avoid confusion with the word *cent* [sQÞ], meaning 'hundred'. However, the two words are pronounced differently, and a parallel situation in Canada (the French word for a hundredth of a Canadian dollar is "cent" [s[nt]) has long existed without attracting attention. Before its use in relation to the euro, the word "cent" pronounced [s[nt] was best known to European Francophones as a hundredth of a known to European Francophones as a hundredth of a dollar (U.S., Canadian, etc.)

In France, the word *centime*, or *centime d'euro*, is far more common than *cent*. According to the Académie Française, "the hundredth of a euro is to be referred to as *centime*".

French-speaking Belgians use more often *cent* than *centime* because *centime* coins for the Belgian franc (worth, on 1 January 1999 about three U.S. cents) rarely circulated (only a 50 centime coin was still being issued) and because of the influence of English, which is more commonly used in Belgium than in France as a result of Belgium's language diversity.

German

Plural: In German, *Euro* and *Cent* are used as both singular and plural when following a numeral, as is the case with all units of measurement of masculine or neuter gender (e.g. *Meter*, *Dollar*, *Kilo(gramm)*, etc.). However, when talking about euros or cents in the sense of individual coins, the plurals *Euros* and *Cents* are used.

The only other marked case is the genitive singular, which is *(des) Euros* or, alternatively, *des Euro*.

Pronunciation: The beginning of the word *Euro* is pronounced in German with the diphthong [Tj], which sounds similar to the 'oi' in the English word "oil".

The spelling of the word *Cent* is not well adapted to German spelling conventions because these strive to avoid ambiguous letter-sound correspondences. Initial letter C is often used in loanwords and pronounced in various ways depending on the language of origin (e.g. [s] in *Centime*, [§] in *Cello*, [¦] in *Celsius* and [k] in *Café*). Most of these words are therefore eventually spelled phonetically (e.g. Kaffee, Kadmium, Zentimeter).

Latin words beginning with "ce" such as *centum* (hundred) are traditionally pronounced [¦] in German, and German words derived from these have therefore for a long time already been spelled with a *Z*, which is pronounced [¦] (as in *Zentrum* (centre), *Zentimeter* (centimetre), etc.). Equivalently, some German speakers pronounce the beginning of the word "Cent" [¦], but since they are familiar with the English pronunciation of the American unit *cent*, most people pronounce it [s].

As these are nouns, both Euro and Cent are capitalised in German.

Slang terms: In Austria and Germany, the euro has also been called *Teuro*, a play on the word *teuer*, meaning 'expensive'. The Deutsche Mark by comparison was worth half as much as the euro (a ratio of approximately 2:1) and some grocers and restaurants are accused of taking advantage of the smaller numbers to increase their actual prices with the changeover.

In youth and Internet culture the fake plural *Euronen* is sometimes used; This form's origin is unknown but it bears resemblance to *Dublonen* (Dubloons) and has a retro ring to it.

In the eastern part of Austria the word *Eumeln* (meaning "twerps", also plural-only) is occasionally used. It combines the word euro with a typical Austrian-German ending (like the word *Semmeln*, Austrian for "bun" or "roll") and gives the word a more casual and familiar touch.

Also, *Öre* is occasionally used, from the Swedish currency.

In German Internet culture, the name *Fragezeichen* (question mark) is occasionally used in reference to the widespread problems with the euro sign which was often rendered as question mark. The term is most often written using the mock currency code FRZ.

Greek

In the Greek language the immutable word *åõñþ* ([evÈro]) is used as the currency's name. It was decided to use omega (ù) rather than omicron (ï) as the last letter of the word, partly because a noun ending with omicron would encourage mutability, and partly to stress the origin of the euro in the Greek word *Åõñþðç* (Europe) which is also spelled with omega and it is actually written on the euro notes in Greek as *ÅÕÑÙ*. Also, the spelling *ÅÕÑÏ* (resulting in a plural *ÅÕÑÁ*) on the notes could have confused other Europeans.

For the cent, the terms used are *ëåðôü*, plural *ëåðôÜ* (*leptó*, plural *leptá*), a name used for small denominations of various ancient and modern Greek currencies, including the drachma (which the euro replaced). The word means 'minute', the same as the unit of measurement of time or of angle.

Although the official term "åõñþ" is indeclinable, some people in spoken Greek say "åõñÜ" (evra) in plural, mostly when making fun of money but not in serious conversation. Also, linguistically speaking, the word "euro" in Greek language functions as a prefix and prefixes don't take plural form. Since there is a word following it (ie. euro-currency), the plural should be put on the potentially present second word. Additionally, the 2 euro ("äýï åõñþ") coin is usually referred to as "äßåõñï" (thievro) by Greeks.

In Cyprus, however, the cent will be called officially

'cent' both in singular and plural. This is the name used now for the 1/100th of the Cyprus pound chosen for its neutrality to both official languages of the Republic (82% of population are Greeks and 18% Turks).

Hungarian

In Hungarian the currency is named *euró* and *cent* (as in Hungarian no plural is used after numbers), the former with a long *ó*, as decided by the Research Institute for Linguistics of the Hungarian Academy of Sciences, since Hungarian words cannot end in short *o* either in writing or in speech (except for one or two interjections), see these international words as examples: *fotó, videó, sztereó*. The spelling is also in accordance with the word "Europe" in Hungarian ("Európa"). The plural is not normally marked in Hungarian after numerals, but both names can take suffixes like *euróval, euróért, euróból*, etc. ("with a euro", "for a euro", "from a euro", etc.).

As of October 2004, Hungary is struggling, along with Lithuania, Latvia, and Slovenia, for the euro to be written in its official documents according to its own usage and spelling, in contrast with a 1998 EU decree which would call for a single name throughout the Union.

The Treaty establishing a Constitution for Europe, signed in 2005, contains the following declaration from Hungary and Latvia:

50. Declaration by the Republic of Latvia and the Republic of Hungary on the spelling of the name of the single currency in the Treaty establishing a Constitution for Europe

Without prejudice to the unified spelling of the name of the single currency of the European Union referred to in the Treaty establishing a Constitution for Europe as displayed on the banknotes and on the coins, Latvia and Hungary declare that the spelling of the name of the single currency, including its derivatives as applied throughout the Latvian and Hungarian text of the Treaty establishing a Constitution for Europe, has no effect on the existing rules of the Latvian and the Hungarian languages.

Icelandic

In Icelandic the euro is called evra, a feminine noun derived from the Icelandic name of Europe, *Evrópa*; this makes Icelandic the only European language in which the word for the euro is feminine. The plural is formed regularly: evrur. The cents are often called sent which is a neuter word and has the same form in the nominative singular. However, a more common usage is to write, say, 20 cents as *0,20 evrur*.

Irish

In Irish, the English words *euro* and *cent* are used, as foreign borrowings without change in spelling or pronunciation, and immune to the regular rules of Irish mutation after numbers. The masculine noun *eoró* (plural *eorónna*) has been coined from the word *Eoraip* ('Europe'), and *ceint* (plural *ceinteanna*) has been in the lexicon since at least 1959. The words *eoró* and *ceint* are attested in printed literature, though the foreign borrowings tend to be more frequent, again due to a lack of coordinated language planning.

Italian

In Italian the word *euro* is used, as both singular and plural. Rarely the word *euri* is used for plural. No slang replacement exists. However the issue of whether the correct plural form would be *euri* or *euro* remained open for a long time, predating the actual introduction of the currency and leaving a relative uncertainty among speakers. The Accademia della Crusca assigned to Severina Parodi, lexicographer, and to Luca Serianni, language historian, the task to give a response. They deliberated in favour of *euri* in 1999 with the motivation that "euro is a masculine noun". But the issue was then re-examined many times. Finally, the consensus of the Accademia was in favour of invariability and appeared, with an articulate rationale, on issue 23 (October 2001) of *La Crusca per voi* (Gli euro e le lingue, (Italian)). The rationale was based on the fact that abbreviated words originating from a longer word (for example *auto* form *automobile* (car) or *moto* from *motocicletta* (motorbike)) do not have a plural form, as well as the fact that the word *Euro* is considered an abbreviation of the word *Europa* (Europe). In the 306th session of the *Senate of the Italian Republic*, December 18, 2002, an amendment to the financial act was proposed to adopt *euri* as the plural form for public official deeds but was quickly rejected (See Amendment 62.5, (Italian)).

The word *cent* is in practical use always replaced by the word *centesimo*, which simply means "hundredth" (also see *centime* in French); its plural form is *centesimi*. *Cent* only appears on documents such as electricity and telephone bills; in any case it is rather perceived by native speakers as an abbreviation of "centesimo" (and in fact often followed by a period and pronounced [§ent]) than as an autonomous proper name.

Latin

In general, according to Latin Wikipedia (Vicipædia), the Living Latin word for euro is the same, euro in the nominative case. In plural, it is eurones in the nominative case.

Due to the inflective nature of the language, it takes the 3rd masculine declension in the five other cases used in the language. They are as follows: in the vocative case, it is *euro* and the plural *eurones*; in the accusative case, it is *euronem* and *eurones*; in the genitive case, it is *euronis* and *euronum*; in the dative case, it is *euronî* and *euronibus*, and finally, in the ablative case, it is *eurone* and *euronibus*.

However, because it does not have the masculine ending, "-us", term euronus, plural euroni, which declines as a 2nd-declension masculine noun, has been used by some speakers.

Latvian

In Latvian there are still at least two concurrent usages. The majority say and write 'eiro' (which somewhat resembles the West European *euro*, but has also taken its sound from *Eiropa*, the Latvian word for *Europe*).

Purists insist that standardised usage is *eira* – a word that is declinable according to the normal and convenient Latvian pattern. *Eirai* clearly means *for the euro*, *eirâs* means *in euros*, and so forth. In contrast, *eiro*, like all Latvian words ending in an '-o', is unable to take on inflections therefore it results in ambiguous phrases like *"samainît eiro"*, which can be interpreted in a variety of ways: *to exchange into euros*, *to exchange euros [for something else]*, *to exchange one euro* – and this limits the fluency of communication.

The official usage of *eira* has been affirmed by Terminology Commission of the Latvian Academy of Sciences, with the argument that a potentially frequently used term needs to fit especially well in the structure of grammar. However, some media outlets and banks have preserved a habit of using *eiro*. Latvian language routinely adapts foreign words by adding declinable endings (like *Òujorka* for New York, *freska* for fresco), although internationalisms ending in '-o' (like *foto*, *auto*) are common as well.

Lithuanian

In Lithuanian the euro and cent are called *euras* and *centas* (in common language usually *eurocentas*, to distinguish from the cents of the current Lithuanian currency, *Litas*), while plural forms are *eurai* and *centai* (*eurocentai*). The Lithuanian language routinely adapts foreign words by re-spelling them according to Lithuanian phonetic rules and adding standardised endings, resulting in words like *kompiuteris* or *Tonis Bleiras*. Lithuania is expected to join the eurozone in 2010.

Maltese

In Maltese euro is spelt *ewro* (in every Maltese text that is not legal), as was announced in December 2005. Ewro is spelled with *w* instead of *u* because it is derived from the Maltese word *Ewropa* (Europe), also written with *w*. Furthermore, the vowels *e* and *u* are not written next to each other in Maltese, except when they are pronounced as two syllables, which is not the case with *Euro*. The plural is unchanged. The cent is known as the *ente¿mu*, plural *ente¿mi*, both abbreviated to .

In Maltese 'ewro' always starts with a small letter *e*, except when it is found in the beginning of a sentence, and ewro is masculine singular.

Norwegian

In Norwegian there could be a problem concerning the spelling, since euro is masculine and would normally take a plural -ar ending in Nynorsk and -er in Bokmål. But since words for foreign currencies (like *dollar* and *yen*) normally do not have the endings -ar or -er in Norwegian the Norwegian Language Council reached a decision in 1996 that the proper conjugation of the word euro should be

in Nynorsk:

ein euro – euroen – euro – euroane

in Bokmål:

en euro – euroen – euro – euroene

The declensions are respectively: The two first in Singular, and the two last in Plural, while the first of each category are indefinite, the last of each category are definite nouns. The word cent is an old loan word in Norwegian – and it is conjugated the same way:

in Nynorsk:

ein cent – centen – cent – centane

in Bokmål:

en cent – centen – cent – centene

The pronunciation of the two words in Norwegian are [È[v.~u] and [s[nt].

Polish

In Polish euro is spelled *euro* in both singular and plural, and pronounced /È[w.rT/. On the other hand *cent* is declinable, being *eurocent* (/[uro¦[nt/) in singular and *eurocenty* (/[uroÈ¦[n.th/) or *eurocentów* (/[uro¦[n.tuf/) in plural.

Portuguese

In Portuguese, *euro* passes as a Portuguese word and thus is used in the singular form, with *euros* as the common plural form. *Cent*, which does not conform to Portuguese word-forming rules, is commonly converted to *cêntimo* (singular) and *cêntimos* (plural).

The term *cêntimo* might have been adopted to distinguish it from the fractional value of the *Portuguese escudo*, which was called *centavo*.

Pronunciation for *euro* in Portuguese is still not standardized, either [Èew.~T] or [Èew.~u], with the former being more widespread in the south of the country, as the latter is in the north.

Some people also call them *ouros* (or the dialectal variation *oiros*) for the resemblance with that Portuguese word meaning "gold".

Romanian

In Romanian the euro and cent are called *euro* and *cent* (plural *ceni*). The official plural of *euro* is also *euro*, and this official form was readily adopted by speakers.

Russian

Russia occupies the largest territory in geographic Europe and is currently the largest holder of the euro currency outside the Eurozone. Russia currently borders on one Eurozone member - Finland, which supplies much of the euro inflow in Russia in trade exchange and tourism, especially to Saint Petersburg. In Russian, just like in the Bulgarian language, euro is spelled *åâðî* both in the singluar and the plural, while *cent* is *öåíò* (sg.) and *öåíòû* (pl.), though there are many colloquial semi-ironic forms such as åâðû 'yevry' based on the similarity with the Russian word åâðåè "yevrei" (Jews), êîïåéêè for cents and others. The same form is used in the singular and the plural. Cents are sometimes transliterated as öåíò 'tsent' - singular, öåíòû 'tsenty' - plural. Numerative form is öåíò for 1 cent (as well as amounts that end in 1 except for the ones ending in 11 - e.g. 51 öåíò but 11 öåíòîâ), öåíòa for 2 to 4 cents (as well as any other amounts ending in 2, 3 or 4, except for the ones ending in 12, 13, 14 - e.g. 54 öåíòa but 12 öåíòoâ) and öåíòoâ for the rest - 88 öåíòoâ. Sometimes eâðîöåíò (also romanized as 'yevrocent' or 'evrotsent') is used to distinguish euro-cents from the American cents.

Serbian

In Serbian the euro and cent are called Serbian Cyrillic: *åâðî* /È[v.ro/ and Serbian Latin *evro* (pl. *åâðà* / *evra*) and *öåíò* / *cent* (pl. *öåíòè* / *centi*). *Evro* is spelled with *v* instead of *u* because it is derived from the word *Åâðîïà* / *Evropa* (Europe), also written with *v*.

The *c* in *cent* is pronounced as /¦/ in accordance with pronunciations in the Serbian language.

In Serbia the Serbian Cyrillic alphabet is official script by the Constitution, the Serbian Latin alphabet is also in use.

Slovak

In Slovak the euro and cent are called *euro* and *cent*, the plural forms for amounts between 2 and 4 are *2 eurá* / *centy*, and the plural forms for larger amounts are *5 eur* / *centov*. *Euro* is spelled with *u* because it is derived from the word *Európa* (Europe).

Slovenian

In Slovenian the euro and cent are called *evro* and

cent, the dual form is *2 evra/centa* and the plural forms are *3 evri/centi* and *5 evrov/centov*. *Evro* is spelled with *v* instead of *u* because it is derived from the word *Evropa* (Europe), also written with *v*.

However, the *v* in the word *evro* is not pronounced as *v*, but as *w* (see Slovenian phonology). The *c* in *cent* is pronounced as ¦.

In laws and regulations, though, the word 'evro' is replaced with the word 'euro' in all grammatical cases in accordance with an agreement between Slovenia and the European Union.

Spanish

In the Spanish language, the official plural is the same as its regular plural *euros*. For the cent, the word *céntimo* (plural *céntimos*) is used. The fraction of the peseta was also called *céntimo*, but no céntimo coins had been issued since 1980, and had since been demonetized. The word "euro" is pronounced as "ewro" in the Spanish language.

Swedish

In Swedish writing, euro(s) as an amount of money is spelt *euro* (and cent is spelt *cent*) both in singular and plural. The currency "the euro" is spelt "euron" following Swedish grammar rules.

In Sweden, officially and used in TV and radio news, it is pronounced [È[v.~u], similarly to how *eu* is pronounced in modern Swedish in *neuro-* or *pseudo-* (but not *Europa* "Europe"). Many people pronounce it in a more English way [ÈjŠĐ.yo] (no "s" in plural). The latter usage is unpopular among purists, who believe English has too much influence on the Swedish language. In Sweden there are no widespread slang terms since the euro is a foreign currency.

In Finland, the euro is the official currency, and Swedish is an official language alongside Finnish. The same spelling as in Sweden is used (officially Swedish in Finland is spelt as in Sweden). The pronunciation, however, is [È[u.~o], which has some similarities to Finnish pronunciation. The abbreviation is like 3,14, same as for Finnish. A common slang term in Finland is "ege", taken from the Finnish language.

Turkish

Turkey and Northern Cyprus continue to use New Turkish Lira as their official currency, but the *euro* is popularly used, particularly by individuals wanting to convert their savings into a more stable currency. The *euro* has colloquially been pronounced in the English fashion since its inception.

In response to criticism of widespread English pronunciation of *euro*, the Turkish Language Association officially introduced *avro* into Turkish ("av" being the first syllable of the Turkish word for Europe, *Avrupa*) in 1998. A concerted campaign by the Turkish Language Association has begun to blossom in recent years, with most sections of the Turkish media now using the new word. It has yet to enter widespread colloquial use, however. The word *avro* could cause problems in the event that Turkey becomes an EU member, and joins euro as the European Commission has refused to allow local variants, unless they are in a different script.

Ukrainian

The euro is becoming relatively widespread in Ukraine although the country doesn't currently border the Eurozone. In standard literary Ukrainian 'euro' is spelt åâðî ('evro'), although Russian-influenced °âðî (pronounced 'yevro') is also possible and more common in large cities across the country, South-Eastern areas, and among Russophones. The same form is used in singular and plural cases. Cents are translated as öåíò ('tsent') - singular, öåíòè ('tsenty') - plural. Like in the Russian language, there is some variation in cases. Numerative form is öåíò for 1 cent (as well as amounts that end in 1 except for the ones ending in 11 - e.g. 51 öåíò but 11 öåíò³â), öåíòè for 2 to 4 cents (as well as any other amounts ending in 2, 3 or 4, except for the ones ending in 12, 13, 14 - e.g. 54 öåíòè but 12 öåíò³â) and öåíò³â for the rest - 88 öåíò³â. Sometimes ºâðîöåíò ('yevrocent') or åâðîöåíò ('evrotsent') is used to distinguish eurocents from American cents.

In constructed languages

In Esperanto, a constructed language, the currency is called "emro", similar to the Esperanto word for the continent "Emropo." A cent is *cendo,* as is commonly used for subunits of all centimalized currency (cents, centimes, etc). The *o* ending in euro conveniently accords with the standard *-o* noun ending in Esperanto, but rather than sound out *e* and *u* separately, Esperanto speakers elected to use the diphthong *em* making the Esperanto name of the currency not identical with what is written on the currency. Plurals are formed in accordance with Esperanto rules, *emroj* and *cendoj*. The words are also declined as any Esperanto noun (emro/emroj in the nominative, emron/emrojn in the accusative). Esperanto speakers are unlikely to call a cent *cento,* since *cento* means 100, rather than a hundredth.

7

Issues in English Phonetics

English phonology is the stud y of the phonology (i.e. the sound system) of the English language. Like all languages, spoken English has wide variation in its pronunciation both diachronically and synchronically from dialect to dialect. This variation is especially salient in English, because the language is spoken over such a wide territory, being the predominant language in Australia, Canada, the Commonwealth Caribbean, Ireland, New Zealand, the United Kingdom and the United States in addition to being spoken as a first or second language by people in countries on every continent, and notably in South Africa and India.

In general the regional dialects of English are mutually intelligible. Although there are many dialects of English, the following are usually used as prestige or standard accents: Received Pronunciation for the United Kingdom, General American for the United States and General Australian for Australia.

Phonemes

The number of speech sounds in English varies from dialect to dialect, and any actual tally depends greatly on the interpretation of the researcher doing the counting. The *Longman Pronunciation Dictionary* by John C. Wells, for example, using symbols of the International Phonetic Alphabet, denotes 24 consonants and 23 vowels used in Received Pronunciation, plus two additional consonants and four additional vowels used in foreign words only. For General American it provides for 25 consonants and 19 vowels, with one additional consonant and three additional vowels for foreign words. The *American Heritage Dictionary*, on the other hand, suggests 25 consonants and 18 vowels (including r-colored vowels) for American English, plus one consonant and five vowels for non-English terms.

Transcription Variants

The choice of which symbols to use for phonemic transcriptions may reveal theoretical assumptions or claims on the part of the transcriber. English 'lax' and 'tense' vowels are distinguished by a synergy of features, such as height, length, and transition (monophthong vs. diphthong); different traditions in the linguistic literature emphasize different ones. For example, if the primary feature is thought to be vowel height, then the non-reduced vowels of General American English.

Although regional variation is very great across English dialects, some generalizations can be made about pronunciation in all (or at least the vast majority) of English accents: Initial-stress-derived nouns mean that stress changes in many English words came about between noun and verb senses of a word. For example, a *rebel* [Èy[.bk)] (stress on the first syllable) is inclined to *rebel* [yj.Èb[k] (stress on the second syllable) against the powers that be. The number of words using this pattern as opposed to only stressing the second syllable in all circumstances doubled every century or so, now including the English words *object*, *convict*, and *addict*.

- The voiceless stops /p t k/ are aspirated at the beginnings of words (for example *tomato*) and at the beginnings of word-internal stressed syllables (for example *potato*).
- A distinction is made between tense and lax vowels in pairs like *beet/bit* and *bait/bet*, although the exact phonetic implementation of the distinction varies from accent to accent. However, this distinction collapses before [K].
- For many people, /r/ is somewhat labialized in some environments, as in *reed* [y·iÐd] and *tree* [ty·iÐ]. In the latter case, the [t] may be slightly labialized as well.
- Wherever /r/ originally followed a tense vowel or diphthong (in Early Modern English) a schwa offglide was inserted, resulting in centering diphthongs like [iY] in *beer* [biYy], [uY] in *poor* [puYy], [ajY] in *fire* [fajYy], [aŠY] in *sour* [saŠYy], and so forth. This phenomenon is known as *breaking*. The subsequent history depends on whether the accent in question is rhotic or not: In non-rhotic accents like RP the postvocalic [y] was dropped, leaving [biY, puY, fajY, saŠY] and the like (now usually transcribed [bjY, pŠY] and so forth). In rhotic accents like General American, on the other hand, the [Yy] sequence was coalesced into a single sound, a non-syllabic [Z], giving [biZ, puZ, fajZ, saŠZ] and the like (now usually transcribed [bjy, pŠy, fajy, saŠy] and so forth). As a result, originally monosyllabic words like those just mentioned came to rhyme with originally disyllabic words like *seer*, *doer*, *higher*, *power*.

- In many (but not all) accents of English, a similar breaking happens to tense vowels before /l/, resulting in pronunciations like [piYk] for *peel*, [puYk] for *pool*, [peYk] for *pail*, and [poYk] for *pole*.
- In many dialects, /h/ becomes [ç] before [j], as in *human* [ÈçjuÐmYn].

Phonotactics

Note: This information applies to RP. Other than variations in the possible onsets with or without final /j/, and the presence or absence of the phoneme, it also applies to the other main varieties of English. It is only occurs syllable-initial and does not occur in clusters.

Syllable Structure

The syllable structure in English is (C)(C)(C)V(C)(C)(C)(C), with a maximal example being *strengths* (/str[Kk¸s/, although it can be pronounced /str[K¸s/).

Onset

There is an on-going sound change (yod-dropping) by which /j/ as the final consonant in a cluster is being lost. In RP, words with /sj/ and /lj/ can usually be pronounced with or without this sound, e.g., [suÐt] or [sjuÐt]. For some speakers of English, including some British speakers, the sound change is more advanced and so, for example, in General American /j/ is also not present after /n/, /l/, /s/, /z/, /¸/, /t/ and /d/. In Welsh English it can occur in more combinations, for example in /tƒj/.

Stress

Stress is phonemic in English. For example, the words *desert* and *dessert* are distinguished by stress, as are the noun *a record* and the verb *to record*. Stressed syllables in

English are louder than non-stressed syllables, as well as being longer and having a higher pitch. They also tend to have a fuller realization than unstressed syllables.

English is a *stress-timed* language. That is, stressed syllables appear at a roughly steady tempo, and non-stressed syllables are shortened to accommodate this.

Examples of stress in English words, using boldface to represent stressed syllables, are *holiday, alone, admiration, confidential, degree,* and *weaker*. Ordinarily, grammatical words (auxiliary verbs, prepositions, pronouns, and the like) do not receive stress, whereas lexical words (nouns, verbs, adjectives, *etc.*) must have at least one stressed syllable.

Traditional approaches describe English as having three degrees of stress: Primary, secondary, and unstressed. However, if stress is defined as relative respiratory force (that is, it involves greater pressure from the lungs than unstressed syllables), as most phoneticians argue, and is inherent in the word rather than the sentence (that is, it is lexical rather than prosodic), then these traditional approaches conflate two distinct processes: Stress on the one hand, and vowel reduction on the other. In this case, primary stress is actually prosodic stress, whereas secondary stress is simple stress in some positions, and an unstressed but not reduced vowel in others. Either way, there is a three-way phonemic distinction: Either three degrees of stress, or else stressed, unstressed, and reduced.

When a stressed syllable contains a pure vowel (rather than a diphthong), followed by a single consonant and then another vowel, as in *holiday,* many native speakers feel that the consonant belongs to the preceding stressed syllable, /ÈhRl.h.dej/, or assign it to both the preceding and following syllables. Such consonants are sometimes describes as *ambisyllabic*. However, when the stressed vowel is a diphthong, as in *admiration* or *weaker,* speakers agree that the consonant belongs to the following syllable: /ÈædmhÈrejƒYn/. (Phonetically, the vowel in *weak* is also a diphthong, [ij].)

Intonation

Prosodic stress is extra stress given to words when they appear in certain positions in an utterance, or when they receive special emphasis. It normally appears on the final stressed syllable in an intonation unit. So, for example, when the word *admiration* is said in isolation, or at the end of a sentence, the syllable *ra* is pronounced with greater force than the syllable *ad*. (This is traditionally transcribed as /ÌædmhÈrejƒYn/.) This is the origin of the primary stress-secondary stress distinction. However, the difference disappears when the word is not pronounced with this final intonation.

Prosodic stress can shift for various pragmatic functions, such as focus or contrast. For instance, consider the dialogue

"Is it brunch tomorrow?"

"No, it's *dinner* tomorrow."

In this case, the extra stress shifts from the last stressed syllable of the sentence, *tomorrow,* to the last stressed syllable of the emphasized word, *dinner.* Compare

"I'm going tomorrow." /ajm ÌaoŠjK tYÈmRroŠ/

or

"I'm going *tomorrow.*" /ajm ÌaoŠjK tYÈÈmRroŠ/

with

"It's *dinner* tomorrow." /jts ÈÈdjnZ tYÌmRroŠ/

Although grammatical words generally do not have lexical stress, they do acquire prosodic stress when emphasized. Compare ordinary

"Come in"! /ÈkŒm jn/

with more emphatic

"Oh, *do* come in!" /oŠ ÈÈduÐ kŒm Ìjn/

History of English Pronunciation

Around the late 14th century, English began to undergo the Great Vowel Shift, in which

- the high long vowels [iÐ] and [uÐ] in words like *price* and *mouth* became diphthongized, first to [Yj] and [YŠ] (where they remain today in some environments in some accents such as Canadian English) and later to their modern values [aj] and [aŠ]. This is not unique to English, as this also happened in Dutch (first shift only) and German (both shifts).

The other long vowels became higher:

- [eÐ] became [iÐ] (for example *meet*),
- [aÐ] became [eÐ] (later diphthongized to [ej], for example *name*),
- [oÐ] became [uÐ] (for example *goose*), and
- [TÐ] become [oÐ] (later diphthongized to [oŠ], for example *bone*).

Later developments complicate the picture: whereas in Geoffrey Chaucer's time *food*, *good*, and *blood* all had the vowel [oÐ] and in William Shakespeare's time they all had the vowel [uÐ], in modern pronunciation *good* has shortened its vowel to [Š] and *blood* has shortened and lowered its vowel to [Œ] in most accents. In Shakespeare's day (late 16th-early 17th century), many rhymes were possible that no longer hold today. For example, in his play *The Taming of the Shrew*, *shrew* rhymed with *woe*.

æ-tensing

æ-tensing is a phenomenon found in many varieties of American English by which the vowel /æ/ has a longer, higher, and usually diphthongal pronunciation in some environments, usually to something like [eY]. Some American accents, for example that of New York City or Philadelphia, make a phonemic distinction between /æ/ and /eY/ although the two occur largely in mutually exclusive environments.

Bad-Lad Split

The bad-lad split refers to the situation in some varieties of southern English English and Australian English, where a long phoneme /æĐ/ in words like *bad* contrasts with a short /æ/ in words like *lad*.

Cot-Caught Merger

The cot-caught merger is a sound change by which the vowel of words like *cot*, *rock*, and *doll* is pronounced the same as the vowel of words like *caught*, *talk*, and *tall*. This merger is widespread in North American English, being found in approximately 40% of American speakers and virtually all Canadian speakers.

Father-Bother Merger

The father-bother merger is the pronunciation of the short O in words such as "bother" identically to the broad A of words such as "father", nearly universal in all of the United States and Canada save New England and the

Maritime provinces; many American dictionaries use the same symbol for these vowels in pronunciation guides.

II

PLAIN LANGUAGE

Plain language is clear, modern, unpretentious language carefully written to ease understanding. It is a reaction to the alleged gobbledygook (aka Legal English) used by lawyers and others to impress or confuse rather than communicate. It distinguishes gobbledygook from useful jargon employed as a shorthand among those who understand it.

Some definitions of plain language are:

- Clear and effective communication. (Professor Joseph Kimble)
- Generally speaking, the idiomatic and grammatical use of language that most effectively presents ideas to the reader. (Bryan Garner)
- Just ... clear, straightforward language, with the needs of the reader foremost in mind. (Michèle Asprey)
- Clear, straightforward expression, using only as many words as are necessary. It is language that avoids obscurity, inflated vocabulary and convoluted construction. It is not baby talk, nor is it a simplified version of ... language. (Dr Robert Eagleson)
- Plain Language is a literary style that is easy-to-read because it matches the reading skill of the audience. (William DuBay)

Ever since ancient times, writers made the distinction between ornate and simple writing. According to Cicero, the plain style is best for instruction. A more elaborate style is proper for entertainment, and the most elegant style for use in formal speeches by attorneys and senators.

Cicero writes that the plain style is not easy. While it may seem close to everyday speech, achieving the effect in formal discourse is a high and difficult art: "plainness of style seems easy to imitate at first thought, but when attempted, nothing is more difficult."

Plainness does not mean the absence of all ornaments, only the more obvious ones. Cicero recognizes what Aristotle had long before pointed out, that a well-turned metaphor or simile can help us see a relation we had not recognized. In fact, he makes abundant use of metaphor and simile to teach us what the plain style is all about:

> ... although it is not full-blooded, it should nevertheless have some of the sap of life so that, though it lack great strength, it may be, so to speak, in sound health.... Just as some women are said to be handsomer when unadorned... so this plain style gives pleasure when unembellished.... All noticeable pearls, as it were, will be excluded. Not even curling irons will be used. All cosmetics, artificial white and red, will be rejected. Only elegance and neatness will remain. (*The Orator,* xxiii, 76-79)

Cicero's teaching about style was to dominate writing until almost our own time. The most famous practitioners of Cicero's plain style included Abraham Lincoln and Mark Twain.

For three hundred years after the Battle of Hastings in 1066, English was the language of the kitchen. By the end of that period, English had dropped its case endings of nouns, personal endings of verbs, and other complexities. Grammar was fixed by word order.

In the six centuries since that time, English has become the language of the greatest body of poetry ever written. Its great prose rivaled that of France. It developed a diversity of literary styles, some of them very ornate, others simple.

By the end of the 1500s, people whose only use of language was to communicate developed a straight-forward style that was free of ornament. It was the language used by merchants, artisans, seamen, and farmers. The more polished language was reserved for the upper and educated classes. Shakespeare was one of the first to parody this pretentious style. See the speeches of Dogberry in *Much Ado About Nothing*. Making fun of people who use fancy language has been a stock device of comedy ever since.

By the end of the 19th century, scholars began studying the features of plain language. In 1893 a Professor of English Literature at the University of Nebraska, A.L. Sherman wrote, *Analytics of Literature: A manual for the objective study of English prose and poetry*. In that work, Sherman showed that the English sentence has shortened over time and that spoken English is a pattern for written English.

Sherman wrote:

> Literary English, in short, will follow the forms of the standard spoken English from which it comes. No man should talk worse than he writes, no man writes better than he should talk.... The oral sentence is clearest because it is the product of millions of daily efforts to be clear and strong. It

represents the work of the race for thousands of years in perfecting an effective instrument of communication. In 1921, the publication of two works, Harry Kitson's "The Mind of the Buyer," and Edward L. Thorndike's "The Teacher's Word Book" picked up where Sherman left off. Kitson's work was the first to apply the principles of empirical psychology to advertising. He advised the use of short words and sentences. Thorndike's work contained the frequency ratings of 10,000 words. He recommended using the ratings in his book to grade books not only for students in schools but also for average readers and adults learning English. Thorndike wrote:

It is commonly assumed that children and adults prefer trashy stories in large measure because they are more exciting and more stimulating in respect to sex. There is, however, reason to believe that greater ease of reading in respect to vocabulary, construction, and facts, is a very important cause of preference. A count of the vocabulary of "best sellers" and a summary of it in terms of our list would thus be very instructive. The 1930s saw an explosion of studies on how to make texts more readable for the average reader. In 1931, Douglas Tyler and Ralph Waples published the results of their two-year study, "What People Want to Read About." In 1934, Ralph Ojemann, Edgar Dale, and Ralph Waples published two studies on writing for adults with limited reading ability. In 1935, educational psychologist William S. Gray teamed up with Bernice Leary to publish their landmark study, "What Makes a Book Readable."

Lyman Bryson at Teachers College in Columbia University led efforts to supply average readers with more books of substance dealing with science and current events. Among Bryson's students were Irving Lorge and Rudolf Flesch, who both became leaders in the plain-language movement.

Others who later led the research in plain language and readability included educator Edgar Dale of Ohio State, Jeanne S. Chall of the Reading Laboratory of Harvard, and George R. Klare of Ohio University. Their efforts spurred the publication of over 200 readability formulas and 1,000 published studies on readability.

Research on what makes a text easy-to-read continues today. Beginning in 1935, a series of literacy surveys showed that the average reader in the U.S. was an adult of limited reading ability. Today, the average adult in the U.S. reads at the 9th-grade level. This is not so surprising when you consider nearly a quarter in the U.S. do not graduate from high school. Drop-outs have an average 3rd-grade reading level. Large numbers graduate from high school reading at the 8th-grade level.

In the 1940s, Robert Gunning and Rudolf Flesch conducted extensive studies of what Americans read. They found that the most popular literature, magazines and pulp fiction, were written at the 7th-grade levels. Today, all popular novels such as *To Kill a Mockingbird* and *The Da Vinci Code* are written at the 7th-grade level. Gunning worked with the United Press and Flesch worked with the Associated Press. They were able to bring down the grade-level of the writing of those organizations from the 16th to the 11th-grade level, where most newspapers remain today.

The plain-language movement has spread to many countries and many languages. There are readability formulas for at least 16 languages besides English, including Spanish, French, German, Chinese, and Vietnamese.

In the 1970s, the consumer-rights movement won legislation that required plain language in contracts, insurance policies, and government regulations. American law schools began requiring students to take legal writing classes which encouraged them to use plain English as much as possible and to avoid legal jargon, except when absolutely necessary. Public outrage with the skyrocketing number of unreadable government forms led to the Paperwork Reduction Act of 1980.

The plain language movement officially started on March 23, 1978, when U.S. President Jimmy Carter signed Executive Order 12044. It said that federal officials must see to it that each regulation is "written in plain English and understandable to those who must comply with it."

In June of 1998, President Bill Clinton issued a memorandum calling for executive departments and agencies to use plain language in all government documents. Vice President Al Gore subsequently spearheaded a plain language initiative that formed a group called the Plain Language Action Network (PLAN) to provide plain language training to government agencies.

III

REGIONAL ACCENTS OF ENGLISH

Local accents are part of local dialects. Any dialect of English has unique features in pronunciation, vocabulary, and grammar. The term "accent" describes only the first of these, namely, pronunciation.

The regional accents of English speakers show great variation across the areas where English is spoken as a first language. This article provides an overview of the many identifiable variations in pronunciation, usually deriving from the phoneme inventory of the local dialect, of the local variety of Standard English between various populations of native English speakers.

Non-native speakers of English tend to carry over the intonation and phonemic inventory from their mother tongue into their English speech. For more details see Non-native pronunciations of English. Among native English speakers, many different accents exist. Some regional accents are easily identified by certain characteristics. It should be noted that further variations are to be found within the regions identified below; for example, towns located less than 10 miles (16 km) from the city of Manchester such as Bolton, Oldham and Salford, each have distinct accents, all of which form the Lancashire accent, yet in extreme cases are different enough to be noticed even by a non-local listener.

There is also much room for misunderstanding between people from different regions, as the way one word is pronounced in one accent (for example, *petal* in American English) will sound like a different word in another accent (for example, *pearl* in Scottish English).

Great Britain

English accents and dialects vary widely in Great Britain. This may be related to the fact that the language has its origins there and has been evolving there for several hundred years. The varieties of English in use in Great Britain are also influenced by the fact that it consists of England, Scotland, and Wales.

England

The main accent groupings within England are between the north and the south; the dividing line runs roughly from Shrewsbury to south of Birmingham and then to The Wash. For many years, the British media and academic bodies have employed Received Pronunciation as a 'standard', although this has become far less common in recent years.

Received Pronunciation has its roots in the speech patterns of south-eastern England. The London-derived Estuary English is now growing in importance as a widespread standard form in the south. There is considerable variation in the accents of the English. Notable geographical accents include West Country (the counties of Cornwall, Devon, Somerset, Dorset, Wiltshire, Gloucestershire and Bristol), North East (Northumberland, Durham, Newcastle, Sunderland), Lancashire (with regional variants in Bolton, Manchester, Blackpool), Merseyside, Yorkshire (which has differences between the North, West and East Ridings), West Midlands (The Black Country, Dudley, Birmingham). The accents of the counties comprising the East Midlands & East Anglia (Nottingham, Derby, Lincoln, Leicester) and (Norfolk, Suffolk, Norwich) some less than 30 miles from the "west midlands" also have a distinct dialect and received pronunciation.

Even within these broad categories there are considerable differences in inflection and pronunciation. The arrival of large scale immigration to England has produced another layer of regional accents that have merged with the accents of immigrants. Such examples include London-Caribbean, West Yorkshire mixed with Pakistani, Indian and Bangladeshi.

Scotland

Wales

The accent of English in Wales is strongly influenced by the phonology of the Welsh language, which more than 20% of the population of Wales speak as their first or second language. North-east Wales sometimes tends to have a Northern English accent due to the large English population on the other side of the border.

Ireland

The differences between accents in the province of Ulster and the remaining three provinces of Ireland are significant enough that it is best to treat them separately. There are, of course, differences within each group as well, but these are often noticeable only to locals.

Ulster

The Ulster accent has two main sub accents, namely Mid Ulster English and Ulster Scots. The language is spoken throughout the nine counties of Ulster, and in some northern areas of bordering counties such as Louth and Leitrim. It bears many similarities to Scottish English through influence from Ulster Scots, which is distinct and recognized as a variety of Scots.

Some characteristics of the Ulster accent include:

- As in Scotland, the vowels /Š/ and /u/ are merged, so that *look* and *Luke* are homophonous. The vowel is a high central rounded vowel, [‰].
- The diphthong /aŠ/ is pronounced approximately [Y‰], but wide variation exists, especially between social classes in Belfast
- The vowel /ej/ is a monophthong in open syllables

(e.g. *day* [d[Ð]) but a rising diphthong in closed syllables (e.g. *daze* [deYz]). But the monophthong remains when inflectional endings are added, thus *daze* contrasts with *days* [d[Ðz].

- The alveolar stops /t, d/ become dental before [r, Z], e.g. *tree* and *spider*
- /t/ often undergoes flapping to [~] before an unstressed syllable, e.g. *eighty* [[Ð~i]

Connaught, Leinster and Munster

The accent of these three provinces is relatively similar throughout, and often distinguishable only by locals or those with experience. To people within the nine counties of Ulster it is more commonly a "southern accent".

Dublin is notable for having accents different from most of the rest of Ireland (although certain other accents are quite distinctive, for example Kerry, Cork, Wexford and Offaly). There is also stereotypically a difference between the accents of the Northside and Southside of Dublin.

Irish Travellers

Irish Travellers have a very distinct accent closely related to a rural Hiberno-English. Many Travellers who were born in parts of Britain have the accent, despite the fact that they do not live in Ireland. They also have their own language which strongly links in with their dialect/ accent of English, see Shelta.

North America

Canada

Three major dialect areas can be found in Canada: Western/Central Canada, the Maritimes, and Newfoundland.

The phonology of West/Central Canadian English, also called *General Canadian*, is broadly identical to that of the Western U.S., except for the following features:

- The diphthongs /aj/ and /aŠ/ are raised to approximately [Yj] and [ŒŠ] before voiceless consonants; thus, for example, the vowel sound of *out* [ŒŠt] is different from that of *loud* [laŠd]. This feature is known as Canadian raising.
- There is no contrast between the vowels of *caught* and *cot* (cot-caught merger); in addition, the short *a* of *bat* is more open than almost everywhere else in North America [æ ~ a]. The other front lax vowels /[/ and /j/, too, can be lowered and/or retracted. This phenomenon has been labelled the Canadian Shift.

With respect to phonemic incidence, the pronunciation of certain words has American and/or British influence. For instance, *shone* is /ƒRn/; *been* is often /bin/; *process* can be either /'pros[s/ or /'prRs[s/; etc.

Words like *drama*, *pyjamas*, *pasta* tend to have /æ/ rather than /Q/ = /R/. Words like *sorrow*, *Florida*, *orange* have /or/ rather than /Qr/; therefore, *sorry* rhymes with *story* rather than with *starry*.

United States

West Indies and Bermuda

For discussion, see:

- Bajan (a creole language)
- Bermudian English
- Caribbean English

- Jamaican English
- Trinidadian English

Southern Hemisphere

Australia

The greatest variation in Australian accents is along educational and occupational lines, expressed as three class-based accents: *Broad Australian*, *General Australian* and *Cultivated Australian*. However, some regional variation has been documented. Generally, accents are found to be broadest in the more remote and rural areas.

A 1995 survey by D. Crystal of the usage of /aĐ/ ("long a") and /æ/ in the same words ("graph", "chance", "demand", "dance", "castle", "grasp" and "contrast", across five cities, found that /aĐ/ was generally strongest in Adelaide, where it was used on average 88% of the time, and weakest in Hobart at 39% (Crystal, 1995, *Cambridge Encyclopedia of the English Language*).

Some people in Victoria have a tendency to pronounce the vowel in words like dress, bed and head as /æ/. As a result, the words "celery" and "salary" are pronounced alike.

In Western Australia, a tendency to pronounce words such as "beer" with two syllables (/biĐ.Y/ or "bɛ-ah"), in cases where other Australians use one syllable (/biY/), has been noted.

According to anecdote and stereotype, Queenslanders tend to use Broad Australian more and to drawl, although this does not appear to have been verified by research, and General and Cultivated accents are also widespread in Queensland.

New Zealand

The New Zealand accent is distinguished from the Australian one by the presence of short or "clipped" vowels, also encountered in South African English. To American ears, the New Zealand soft "s" sounds slushy, more like "sh", so that "consumer" sounds like "con-SHOO-mer". This is attributable to the influence of Scottish English speech patterns. The Scottish English influence is more evident in the southern regions of New Zealand, notably Dunedin.

Geographical variations appear slight, and mainly confined to individual special local words. One group of speakers, however, hold a recognised place as "talking differently": the South of the South Island (Murihiku) harbours a "Celtic fringe" of people speaking with a "Southland burr" in which a back-trilled 'r' appears prominently. The area formed a traditional repository of immigration from Scotland.

The trilled 'r' is also used by some Mâori, who may also pronounce 't' and 'k' sounds almost as 'd' and 'g'. This is also encountered in South African English, especially among Afrikaans speakers.

South Atlantic

Saint Helena

"Saints", as Saint Helenan islanders are called, have a variety of different influences on their accent. To outsiders, the accent has resemblances to the accents of South Africa, Australia, and New Zealand. Television is a reasonably recent arrival there, and is only just beginning to have an effect.

Falkland Islands

The Falkland Islands have a large non-native born

population, mainly from England, but also from Saint Helena. In rural areas, the Falkland accent tends to be stronger. The accent has resemblances to both Australia-NZ English, and that of Norfolk in England, and contains a number of Spanish loanwords.

Southern Africa

South Africa

South Africa has 11 official languages, one of which is English. Afrikaners (Boers), descendants of mainly Dutch settlers, tend to pronounce English phonemes with a strong Afrikaans inflection, which is very similar to Dutch.

Native English speakers in South Africa have an accent that generally resembles British Received pronunciation modified with varying degrees of Germanic inflection (caused by the Afrikaner influence). Native English speakers in South Africa also insert varying numbers of Afrikaans and Zulu loanwords into their speech.

British people often confuse South African English with Australian English while Americans often confuse it with an Upper Class British accent.

The accents of native English speakers of Johannesburg differ. Those from the northern suburbs (Parkview, Parkwood, Parktown North, Saxonwold, etc) tend to be less strongly influenced by Afrikaans. These suburbs are populated by persons with tertiary education and higher incomes. The accents of native English speakers from the southern suburbs (Rosettenville, Turffontein, etc) tend to be more strongly influenced by Afrikaans. These suburbs are populated by tradesmen and factory workers, with lower incomes. The extent of Afrikaans influence is explained by the fact that Afrikaans urbanisation would historically have been from failed marginal farms or failing economies in rural towns, into the southern and western suburbs of Johannesburg. The western suburbs of Johannesburg (Newlands, Triomf, which has now reverted to its old name Sophiatown, Westdene, etc) are predominantly Afrikaans speaking.

Zimbabwe

In Zimbabwe, native English speakers (mainly the white minority) have a similar speech pattern to that of South Africa. Hence those with high degrees of Germanic inflection would pronounce 'Zimbabwe' as *zom-baw-bwi*, as opposed to the African pronunciation *zeem-bah-bwe*.

Namibia

Namibian English tends to be strongly influenced by that of South Africa.

Asia

Hong Kong

The accent of English spoken in Hong Kong follows mainly British, with rather strong influence from Cantonese on the pronunciations of a few consonants and vowels, and sentence grammar and structure. In recent years there are some Canadian and Australian influences, attributable to the return to Hong Kong of persons who had emigrated to these countries.

South Asia

A number of distinct dialects of English are spoken in South Asia. Accents originating in this part of the world tend to display several distinctive features, including:

- syllable-timing, in which a roughly equal time is

allocated to each syllable. Akin to the English of Singapore and Malaysia. (Elsewhere, English speech timing is based predominantly on stress);

- "sing-song" pitch (somewhat reminiscent of those of Welsh English).

Malaysia and Singapore

English is the lingua franca of Malaysia and Singapore, two former British colonies. It also is the most frequently used language in the homes of about 23% of Singaporeans.

The Singaporean and Malaysian accents are fairly similar and the distinctions between the two are analogous to that between the American and Canadian accents. The Singaporean/Malaysian accent is so distinctive that it is one of the ways Singaporeans and Malaysians recognize one another when they are overseas.

The Singaporean/Malaysian accent appears to be a melding of British, Chinese, and Malay influences.

Many Singaporeans and Malaysians adopt different accents and usages depending on the situation, for example an office worker may speak with less colloquialism and with a more British accent at the job than with friends or while out shopping.

- syllable-timing, where speech is timed according to syllable, akin to the English of the Indian Subcontinent. (Elsewhere, speech is usually timed to stress.)
- A quick, staccato style, with "puncturing" syllables and well-defined, drawn out tones.
- No rhotic vowels, like British English. Hence "caught" and "court" rhyme, both being pronounced /kTĐt/, "can't" rhymes with "aren't", etc.

- Much dropping off of final consonants: "must" becomes "mus'", "cold" becomes "co'", etc.
- The "ay" and "ow" sounds in "raid" and "road" (/ej/ and /oŠ/ respectively) are pronounced as monophthongs, i.e. with no "glide": /red/ and /rod/.
- /¸/ is pronounced as /t/ and /ð/ as /d/; hence, "thin" is /tjn/ and "then" is /d[n/.
- Depending on how colloquial the situation is: many discourse particles, or words inserted at the end of sentences that indicate the role of the sentence in discourse and the mood it conveys, like "lah", "leh", "mah", "hor", etc.
- The main shiboleth for distinguishing a Singaporean and a Malaysian would be the pronunciation of the word "Malaysia." A Singaporean is more likely to say "Malay-zhuh", while a Malaysian would more likely say "Malayss-syuh."

Philippines

Philippine English is heavily influenced by American English but it is also influenced by Tagalog and other Philippine languages.

Many vowels and consonant sounds such as [f] and [v] or [e] and [i] are interchanged frequently Philippine languages so they are realized differently by Filipinos.

- Filipino: [pilipino]
- Victor: [biktor]
- Family: [pamili]
- Varnish: [barnis]
- Fun: [pan]
- Vehicle: [bihikel]

- Lover = [laber]
- Find = [paInd]
- Official: [opisyal]
- Very = [beri]

Currently, Filipinos are more sensitive to pronunciation due to their large exposure to English movies and books. English is also the second language in the Philippines and it is used as the medium of around 80% of the schools' subjects. Also, due to the vast entry of business processes outsourcing (BPO) companies like call centers, English tutorial schools and medical transcription companies; it was an avenue to the improvement and utilization of the English language and its pronunciation.

IV

RHOTIC AND NON-RHOTIC ACCENTS

English pronunciation is divided into two main accent groups, the rhotic and non-rhotic, depending on when the sound typically represented in spelling with the letter R is pronounced. (The word *rhotic* is pronounced /ÈroŠtjk/ in General American and /ÈrYŠtjk/ in RP.) Rhotic speakers pronounce written /r/ in all positions, while non-rhotic speakers pronounce /r/ only if it is followed by a vowel sound (see "linking and intrusive R"), and not always even then. In linguistic terms, non-rhotic accents are said to exclude the phoneme /r/ from the syllable coda. This is commonly referred to as the post-vocalic R, although that term can be misleading because not all Rs that occur after vowels are excluded in non-rhotic English.

Development

The earliest traces of a loss of /r/ in English are found

in the environment before /s/ in spellings from the mid-15th century: the Oxford English Dictionary reports *bace* for earlier *barse* (today "bass", the fish) in 1440 and *passel* for *parcel* in 1468. In the 1630s, the word *juggernaut* is first attested, which represents the Hindi word *jagannâth*, meaning "lord of the universe". The English spelling uses the digraph *er* to represent a Hindi sound close to the English schwa. Loss of coda /r/ apparently became widespread in southern England during the 18th century; John Walker uses the spelling *ar* to indicate the broad A of *aunt* in his 1775 dictionary and reports that *card* is pronounced "caad" in 1791 (Labov, Ash, and Boberg 2006: 47).

Non-rhotic speakers pronounce the [y] in *red*, and most pronounce it in *torrid* and *watery* (in each case the [y] is followed by a vowel) but not the written R of *hard*, nor that of *car* or *water*. However, in most non-rhotic accents, if a word ending in written "r" is followed closely by another word beginning with a vowel, the [y] is pronounced—as in *water ice*. This phenomenon is referred to as "linking R". Many non-rhotic speakers also insert epenthetic [y]s between vowels when the first vowel is one that can occur before syllable-final *r* (*drawring* for *drawing*). This so-called "intrusive R" is frowned upon by those who use the non-rhotic Received Pronunciation but even they frequently "intrude" an epenthetic [y] at word boundaries, especially where one or both vowels is schwa; for example *the idea of it* becomes *the idea-r-of it*, *Australia and New Zealand* becomes *Australia-r-and New Zealand*. The typical alternative used by RP speakers is to insert a glottal stop where an intrusive R would otherwise be placed.

For non-rhotic speakers, what was historically a vowel plus [y] is now usually realized as a long vowel. So *car*, *hard*, *fur*, *born* are phonetically /kQĐ/, /hQĐd/, /f\Đ/, / bTĐn/. This length is retained in phrases, so *car owner* is /kQĐyYŠnY/. But a final schwa remains short, so *water* is /wTĐtY/. The vowels /iĐ/ and /uĐ/ (or /Š/), when followed by *r*, become diphthongs ending in schwa, so *near* is /njY/ and *poor* is /pŠY/. The same happens to diphthongs followed by R (or they end in /Z/ in rhotic speech and that sound turns into a schwa as usual in non-rhotic speech): *tire* is / tajY/ and *sour* is /saŠY/ (*New Shorter Oxford English Dictionary*). For some speakers some long vowels alternate with a diphthong ending in schwa, so *wear* is /w[Y/ but *wearing* is /w[ĐyiK/. Some pairs of words with distinct pronunciations in rhotic accents are homophones in many non-rhotic accents. Examples in Received Pronunciation include *father* and *farther*; *draws* and *drawers*; *formally* and *formerly*; *area* and *airier*. In Australian English, which has the weak vowel merger, pairs like *batted/battered* or *boxes/boxers* are homophones. Syllabication interacts with rhoticity: *sheer* and *Shi'a* respectively have one and two syllables; in some non-rhotic speech, this may be insufficient for distinguishing them.

Distribution

Examples of rhotic accents are: Mid-Ulster English and General American. Non-rhotic accents include Received Pronunciation, and Australian, South African and Estuary English.

Most speakers of American English are rhotic. Outside the United States, rhotic accents can be found in Barbados, Canada, Ireland and Scotland. In England, rhotic accents are found in the West Country, the Corby area and most of Lancashire; they were traditionally across the whole of Lancashire and bordering parts of Yorkshire, Northumberland and rural parts of south-east England, although the younger generation are more likely to be non-rhotic in these areas. Other areas with rhotic accents include Otago and Southland in the far south of New Zealand's South Island, where a Scottish influence is apparent.

Areas with non-rhotic accents include Australia, most of the Caribbean, most of England (notably Received Pronunciation speakers), most of New Zealand, Wales, and Singapore.

Canada is entirely rhotic except for small isolated areas in southwestern New Brunswick, parts of Newfoundland, and Lunenburg and Shelburne Counties, Nova Scotia.

In the United States, large parts of the South were formerly non-rhotic, but this is sharply recessive. Today, non-rhoticity in Southern American English is found primarily among older speakers, and only in some areas such as New Orleans (known endearingly as the Yat accent), southern Alabama, Savannah, Georgia, and Norfolk, Virginia (Labov, Ash, and Boberg 2006: 47–48). Parts of New England, especially Boston, are non-rhotic as well as New York City and surrounding areas. The case of New York is especially interesting because of a classic study in sociolinguistics by William Labov showing that the non-rhotic accent is associated with older and middle- and lower-class speakers, and is being replaced by the rhotic accent. African American Vernacular English (AAVE) is largely non-rhotic.

There are a few accents of Southern American English where intervocalic [y] is deleted before an unstressed syllable and at the end of a word even when the following word begins with a vowel. In such accents, pronunciations like [kæYlaÐnY] for *Carolina* and [b[ÐŒp] for "bear up" are heard (Harris 2006: 2–5). These pronunciations also occur in AAVE (Pollock et al. 1998)

In Asia, the Philippines is the paramount example of rhotic dialect. This may be explained because the English that is spken here is heavily influenced by the American dialect.

Similar Phenomena in Other Languages

The rhotic consonant is dropped or vocalised under similar conditions in other Germanic languages, notably German, Danish and some dialects of southern Sweden (possibly due to the proximity to Denmark). In most varieties of German, /r/ in the syllable coda is frequently realised as a vowel or a semivowel, [P] or [P/], especially in the unstressed ending *-er* and after long vowels: for example *sehr* [zeÐP/], *besser* [Èb[sP]. Similarly, Danish /r/ after a vowel is, unless preceded by a stressed vowel, either pronounced as [P/] (*mor* "mother" [moP/À], *næring* "nourishment" [Èn[P/eK]) or merged with the preceding vowel while usually influencing its quality (/a(Ð)r/ and / TÐr/ / /Tr/ are realised as long vowels [aÐ] and [RÐ], and /Yr/, /rY/ and /rYr/ are all pronounced as [P]) (*løber* "runner" [ÈløÐb%P], *Søren Kierkegaard* (personal name) [ÌsœÐPn Èk°iP/gYÌgRÐÀ]).

Among the Turkic languages, Uyghur displays more or less the same feature, as syllable-final /r/ is dropped, while the preceding vowel is lengthened: for example *Uyghurlar* ["Šj'•ŠÐlaÐ] 'Uyghurs'. The /r/ may, however, sometimes be pronounced in unusually "careful" or "pedantic" speech; in such cases, it is often mistakenly inserted after long vowels even when there is no phonemic /r/ there. Similarly in Yaqui, an indigenous language of northern Mexico, intervocalic or syllable-final /r/ is often dropped with lengthening of the previous vowel: *pariseo* becomes /pa:áseo/, *sewaro* becomes /sewajo/.

In some dialects of Brazilian Portuguese, word-final /r/ is unpronounced or becomes simply an aspiration (mostly in interior of Minas Gerais, São Paulo, Paraná and Mato Grosso do Sul states), while in Thai, pre-consonantal /r/ is unpronounced.

Effect on Spelling

Non-rhotic pronunciation can affect phonetic spelling of dialectal or foreign words. In addition to *juggernaut* mentioned above, the following are found:

- British English slang words:
  - "char" for "cha" from the Mandarin Chinese pronunciation of 6*f* (= "tea" (the drink))
  - "nark" (= "informer") from Romany "nâk" (= "nose").
- In Rudyard Kipling's books:
  - "dorg" instead of "dawg" for a drawled pronunciation of "dog".
  - Hindu Indian god name Kama misspelled as "Karma".
  - Hindustani > " < "kâgaz" (= "paper") spelled as "kargaz".

V

NON-NATIVE PRONUNCIATIONS OF ENGLISH

Non-native pronunciations of English result from speakers of any language (other than English) imperfectly learning the pronunciation of English, either by transferring the phonological rules from their mother tongue into their

English speech ("interference") or by implementing strategies similar to those used in primary language acquisition. They may also create innovative pronunciations for English sounds not found in the speaker's first language. The age at which speakers begin to immerse themselves into a language (such as English) is linked to the degree in which native speakers are able to detect a non-native accent; the exact nature of the link is disputed amongst scholars and may be affected by "neurological plasticity, cognitive development, motivation, psychosocial states, formal instruction, language learning aptitude," and the usage of their first (L1) and second (L2) languages.

More transparently, differing phonological distinctions between a speaker's first language and English create a tendency to neutralize such distinctions in English and differences in the inventory or distribution of sounds may cause substitutions of native sounds in the place of difficult English sounds and/or simple deletion. This is more common when the distinction is subtle between English sounds or between a sound of English and of a speaker's primary language; nevertheless, there is no evidence to suggest that a simple absence of a sound or sequence in one language's phonological inventory makes it difficult to learn.

In addition, the grammar differences (for example the differences in tense, number, gender, etc.) in different languages often lead to grammatical mistakes. The English dialect in which second language learners are exposed to may also be a factor. In some places that were formerly under British rule, such as India, Hong Kong and Malaysia the English language remains a mandatory subject in the schools and the accents of such students show influences in vocabulary, grammar, and pronunciation from British English.

Such characteristics may be transmitted to the children of bilinguals, who will then exhibit a number of the same characteristics even if they are monolingual.

Non-native accents by region in alphabetical order:

Arabic

- Speakers tend to speak with a rhotic accent and pronounce /r/ as a flap or trill.

Chinese

- Because Chinese lacks any overt number category, speakers of Chinese frequently combine a plural subject with a singular verb or vice versa.

German

- Speakers may not velarize /l/ in coda positions as native speakers do.

See also: German phonology

Hungarian

- The dental fricatives /¸/ and /ð/ may be replaced by [s;] and [d*]

Italian

A study on Italian children's pronunciation of English revealed the following characteristics:

- Tendency to replace the English high lax vowels / j/ /Š/ with [i] [u] (ex: "fill" and "feel", "put" "poot" are homophones), since Italian doesn't have these vowels.
- Tendency to replace /K/ with [Kg] ("singer" rhymes with "finger") or as [n] (combined with the above tendency makes the words "king" and "keen" homophones) because Italian [K] is an allophone of /n/ before velar stops.

- Tendency to replace word-initial /sm/ with [zm], e.g. *small* [zmTl].
- Tendency to replace /Œ/ with [a] so that *mother* is pronounced [ÈmadYr] or [ÈmaðYr].
- Italian does not have dental fricatives:
  - Voiceless /¸/ may be replaced with a dental [t*] or with [f].
  - Voiced /ð/ may become a dental [d*].
- Since /t/ and /d/ are typically pronounced as dental stops anyway, words like *there* and *dare* can become homophones.
- /æ/ is replaced with [[], so that *bag* sounds like *beg* [b[g].
- Tendency to pronounce /p t k/ as unaspirated stops.
- Schwa [Y] does not exist in Italian; speakers tend to give the written vowel its full pronunciation, e.g. *lemon* [Èl[mRn], *television* [t[leÈvi'Rn], *parrot* [Èpærot], *intelligent* [inÈt[lid'[nt], *water* [ÈwTt[r], *sugar* [Èƒugar].
- Italian speakers may pronounce consonant-final English words with a strong vocalic offset, especially in isolated words, e.g. *dog* [dRgJ"]. This has led to the stereotype of Italians adding [Y] to the ends of English words.
- Tendency to pronounce /r/ as a trill [r] rather than the English approximant /y/, e.g. *parrot* [Èpærot].

In addition, Italians learning English have a tendency to pronounce words as they are spelled, so that *walk* is [wRlk], *guide* is [gwid], and *boiled* is [ÈbTjl[d]. This is also true for loanwords borrowed from English as *water*, which is pronounced as [vat[r] instead of [ÈwTĐtY]. Related to this is the fact that many Italians produce /r/ wherever it is spelled (e.g. *star* [star]), resulting in a rhotic accent, even when the dialect of English they are learning is nonrhotic. Consonants written double may be pronounced as geminates, e.g. Italians pronounce *apple* with a longer [p] sound than English speakers do.

Russian

- There is no /w/ in Russian; speakers typically substitute [v] and will have trouble perceiving the difference between the two.
- Russian does not have the dental fricatives [,] and [ð], so they may be replaced with alveolar fricatives or dental stops.
- Alveolar consonants /s/ /d/ /t/ /n/ may be pronounced as dental.
- Russian has only five or six vowels phonemes and speakers may have trouble with vowels not in their native inventories.
  - /[/ and /æ/ are pronounced as the former. E.g. "man" and "men" are pronounced [m[n].
  - The diphthongs /aj/, /ej/, and /Tj/ sound with the consonant [j] sound instead of the short / j/. E.g. "high" sounds like [haj], rather than [haj].

Spanish

- Since Spanish does not make voicing contrasts between its fricatives (and its one affricate), speakers may neutralize contrasts between /s/ and /z/; likewise, fricatives may assimilate the voicing of a following consonant.

- Speakers tend to merge /tʃ/ with /ʃ/, and /d'/ and / '/ with /j/.
- /j/ and /w/ often have a fluctuating degree of closure.
- For the most part (especially in colloquial speech), Spanish allows only five (or six) word-final consonants: /s/, /n/, /~/, /l/ and /d/ (plus /¸/ in Northern Peninsular Spanish); speakers may omit word-final consonants other than these.
- In Spanish, /s/ must immediately precede or follow a vowel; often a word beginning with [s] + consonant will obtain an epenthetic vowel (typically [e]) to make *stomp* pronounced as [esÈtQmp] rather than [stQmp].
- In Spanish, a voiceless dental fricative /¸/ phoneme exists only in the Northern Peninsular dialect; where this sound appears in English, speakers of other Spanish dialects substitute /t/, /s/ or /f/ for it.
- Speakers tend to merge /ð/ and /d/, pronouncing both as voiced dental plosive unless they occur in intervocalic position, in which case they are pronounced as [ð]. A similar process occurs with /v/ and /b/.
- The three nasal phonemes of Spanish neutralize in coda-position; speakers may invariably pronounce nasal consonants as homorganic to a following consonant; if word-final (as in *welcome*) common realizations include [n], deletion with nasalization of the preceding vowel, or [K].

Vietnamese

Note: There are two main dialects in Vietnamese, a northern one centered around Hanoi and a southern one centered around Ho Chi Minh City.

- Speakers may not produce final consonants since there are fewer final consonants in Vietnamese and those that do exist differ in their phonetic quality:
  - Final /b/ is likely to be confused with /p/
  - Final /d/ is likely to be confused with /t/
  - Final /f/ is likely to be confused with /p/
  - Final /v/ is likely to be confused with /b/ or /p/
  - Final /s/ is likely to be confused with /ʃ/ or simply omitted
  - Final /ʃ/ is likely to be omitted
  - Final /z/ is likely to be confused with /ʃ/ or /s/
  - Final /tʃ/ is likely to be confused with /ʃ/
  - Final /l/ is likely to be confused with /n/
- Speakers also have difficulty with English consonant clusters, with segments being omitted or epinthetic vowels being inserted.
- Speakers may not aspirate initial /t/ and /k/, making (American) listeners perceive them as /d/ and /g/ respectively.
- Speakers often have difficulty with the following phonemes:
  - /¸/, which is confused with /t/ or /s/
  - /ð/, which is confused with /d/ or /z/
  - /p/, which is confused with /b/
  - /g/, which is confused with /k/
  - /d’/, which is confused with /z/
  - /’/, which is confused with /z/ or /d’/
  - /s/, which is confused with /ʃ/

- /ty/, which is confused with /d'/, /tʃ/ or /t/
- /v/, which is confused with /j/
- /j/, which is confused with /i/
- /Š/, which is confused with /u/ or /Œ/
- /[/, which is confused with /æ/
- /æ/, which is confused with /[/ or /Q/

- Vietnamese is a tonal language and speakers may try to use the Vietnamese tonal system or use a monotone with English words. They may also associate tones onto the intonational pattern of a sentence and becoming confused with such inflectional changes.

VI

PRONUNCIATION RESPELLING FOR ENGLISH

Respelling systems were designed for native speakers of English, and they copy standard English spelling as closely as possible. This makes it unnecessary for the dictionary user to learn the IPA.

Dictionaries and other language reference works usually provide a pronunciation guide for the words that they list. Most current British English dictionaries use the International Phonetic Alphabet (IPA) for this purpose. The pronunciation which these dictionaries refer to is the so-called *received pronunciation*, which is based upon educated speech in southern England. But most American dictionaries, and some British ones, use a respelling system that is more intuitive than the IPA.

The IPA system is not a respelling system because it uses symbols such as ð and è which are not used in English spelling.

Traditional Respelling Systems

The following chart matches the IPA symbols used to represent the sounds of the English language with the phonetic symbols used in several dictionaries, a majority of which transcribe American English.

The works referenced above adhere (for the most part) to the one-symbol-per-sound principle. Other works not included here, such as *Webster's New Twentieth Century Dictionary of the English Language* (unabridged, 2nd ed.), do not and thus have several different symbols for the same sound (partly to allow for different phonemic mergers and splits).

International Phonetic Alphabet

The International Phonetic Alphabet is a standardized method of phonetic transcription developed by a group of English and French language teachers in 1888. In the beginning, only specialized pronunciation dictionaries for linguists used it, for example, the *English Pronouncing Dictionary* edited by Daniel Jones (EPD, 1917). The IPA was used by English teachers as well, and started to appear in popular dictionaries for learners of English as a foreign language, such as the *Oxford Advanced Learner's Dictionary* (1948), and *Longman Dictionary of Contemporary English* (1978).

IPA is very flexible, allowing for a wide variety of transcriptions between broad phonemic transcriptions which describe the significant units of meaning in language, and phonetic transcriptions which indicate every nuance sound in detail. The IPA pronunciation scheme used in the first twelve editions of the EPD was relatively simple, using a *quantitative* system indicating vowel length using a colon, and requiring the reader to infer other vowel qualities.

Many phoneticians preferred a *qualitative* system, which used different symbols to indicate vowel timbre and colour. A.C. Gimson introduced a *quantitative-qualitative* IPA notation system when he took over editorship of the EPD (13th edition, 1967), and by the 1990s, the Gimson system had become a de facto standard for phonetic notation of British Received Pronunciation (RP).

Comparison of Short and Long Vowels in Various IPA Schemes for RP

word	*quant.*	*qual.*	*Gimson*
cod	kTd	kRd	kRd
cord	kT:d	kTd	kT:d
rid	rid	rjd	rjd
reed	ri:d	rid	ri:d

The first native (not learner's) English dictionary using IPA may have been the *Collins English Dictionary* (1979), and others followed suit. The *Oxford English Dictionary*, 2nd edition (OED2, 1989) used IPA, transcribed letter-for-letter from entries in the first edition, which had been noted in a scheme by the original editor, James Murray.

While IPA has not been adopted by popular dictionaries in the United States, there is a demand for learner's dictionaries which provide both British and American English pronunciation. Some dictionaries, such as the *Cambridge English Pronouncing Dictionary* and the *Longman Dictionary of Contemporary English* provide a separate transcription for each.

British and American English dialects have a similar set of phonemes, but some are pronounced differently; in technical parlance, they consist of different phones. Although developed for RP, the Gimson system being phonemic, it is not far from much of General American pronunciation as well. A number of recent dictionaries, such as the *Collins COBUILD Advanced Learner's English Dictionary*, add a few non-phonemic symbols /r i u Yl Yn/ to represent both RP and General American pronunciation in a single IPA transcription.

Adaptations of the Gimson system for American English

/R/ Pronounced [Q:] in General American.

/e/ In American English falls between [e] and [æ] (sometimes transcribed /[/)

/Yu/ This traditional transcription is probably more accurately replaced by /ou/ in American English.

/r/ Regular r is always pronounced

/r/ Superscript r is only pronounced in rhotic dialects, such as General American, or when followed by a vowel (for example adding a suffix to change *dear* into *dearest*)

/i/ *Medium i* can be pronounced [j] or [i:], depending on the dialect

/T:/ Many Americans pronounce /T:/ the same as /R/ ([Q:])

/Yl/ Syllabic l, sometimes transcribed /l/ or /Yl/

/Yn/ Syllabic n, sometimes transcribed /n/ or /Yn/

Clive Upton updated the Gimson scheme, changing the symbols used for five vowels. He served as pronunciation consultant for the influential *Concise Oxford English Dictionary*, which adopted this scheme in its ninth edition (1995). Upton's reform is controversial: it reflects changing pronunciation, but critics say it represents a narrower regional accent, and abandons parallelism with American and Australian English

Upton's Reform

word	*Gimson*	*Upton*
bet	bet	b[t
bat	bæt	bat
nurse	n\:s	nY:s
square	skweY	skw[:
price	prajs	prŒjs

The in-progress 3rd edition of the Oxford English Dictionary uses Upton's scheme for representing British pronunciations. For American pronunciations it uses an IPA-based scheme devised by Prof. William Kretzschmar of the University of Georgia.

8

Theories of Communicative Competence

No doubt, the role of input is of critical importance in understanding the what and why of second language acquisition. To this end, we are seeing an increasing number of studies which focus on fine-grained analyses of the nature of foreigner talk, teacher talk and learner talk, as well as on the variables intervening between input and intake.

The data base for the majority of these studies is input to learners of English as a second or foreign language, and input to adults.

The focus of this chapter, and the data base employed, are considerably different. Rather than focusing on a micro-analysis of learner input in specific interactional events, attention will be paid to the input-output relationship at the level of language proficiency *traits,* specifically the traits of grammatical, discourse annnd sociolinguistic competence.

The data come from children whose first language is English, and who are learning French as a second language in the school setting of a French immersion programme. Compared with ESL learners, these children make infrequent use of the target language outside of the school setting. Thus, the second language input to these students is largely that of native-speaker teacher talk and non-native peer talk, as well as, of course, experience with literacy activities. Within a theoretical framework that incorporates traits and contexts of language use, the structure of the immersion students' output, that is, the structure of their language proficiency can be seen to relate rather directly to the nature of the input received. However, aspects of the immersion students' second language proficiency cannot be totally accounted for on the basis of the input received. This chapter, then, will consider the second language proficiency exhibited by these French immersion students, relating their output at a macro level to their language learning environment. Of the conclusions I will draw, one that I think is fundamental to our understanding of the role of input in second language acquisition, is that although comprehensible input (Krashen 1981, 1982) may be essential to the acquisition of a second language, it is not enough to ensure that the outcome will be native-like performance. In fact, I will argue that while comprehensible input and the concomitant emphasis on interaction in which meaning is negotiated (e.g. Long 1983; Varonis and Gass 1985) is essential, its impact on grammatical development has been overstated.

The role of these interactional exchanges in second language acquisition may have as much to do with 'comprehensible output,' as it has to do with comprehensible input. The data I will be drawing on in this chapter come from one study undertaken within the context of a large-scale research project concerned with the development of bilingual proficiency. The overall aim of the research is to explore the influences of social, educational and individual variables on the processes and outcomes of second language learning. The specific goal of the study I will be discussing here was to determine the extent to which certain components of language proficiency represented in our theoretical framework as linguistic traits were empirically distinguishable, and were differentially manifested in oral and written tasks.

Other studies currently underway as part of the same large-scale research programme will compare the structure of language proficiency of French immersion students with that of other learners who have learned their second language under considerably different conditions. Thus, although of theoretical interest, the research programme has been designed to have direct bearing on language policy issues in schools through the identification of strengths and weaknesses in certain aspects of the students' language proficiency. The basic theoretical framework within which the study was carried out is diagrammed in Figure 1. The framework incorporates as traits several components of communicative competence proposed by Canale and Swain (1980a) and Canale (1983) — grammatical, discourse and sociolinguistic; and incorporates as methods, oral and literacy based tasks.

For each cell in the matrix of traits by methods shown in Figure 1, a test and relevant scoring procedures were developed. The details of the tests, scoring procedures and reliability indices are described elsewhere (Allen *et al.* 1982, 1983). Here, I will confine myself to a brief trait-by-trait description of the tests and main features of the scoring procedures utilized. The scoring breakdown has theoretical interest in that it pinpoints which aspects of language competence are being assessed in each test.

FIGURE 1

		Traits	
	Grammar	*Discourse*	*Sociolinguistic*
Oral production	structured interview	film retelling and argumentation	— requests — suggestions — complaints
Multiple choice	45 items	29 items	28 items
Written production	<—————— <——————	2 Narratives 2 letters ———————	2 notes ——> directives

The trait of grammatical competence was operationalized as rules of morphology and syntax, with a major focus on verbs and prepositions. The oral production task consists of a structured interview which embeds thirty-six standardized questions in a conversation. The topics are concrete and familiar, designed to focus the student's attention on communication rather than on the second language code.

The standardized questions are designed to elicit a range of verb forms and prepositions in French, as well as responses that are sufficiently elaborated to score of syntactic accuracy. Grammatical scoring, then, was based on the student's ability to use certain grammatical forms accurately in the context of particular questions. The grammatical multiple choice test consists of forty-five items assessing knowledge of similar aspects of syntax and morphology as were elicited in the interview situation.

In the grammatical written production tasks the student is presented with four situations and asked to write a short text about each. The four topics were designed to bias towards the use of the past and present tenses through two narrations, and future and conditional tenses through two letters of request.

Grammatical errors were tallied for each of four categories: syntactic errors, preposition errors, homophonous verb errors and non-homophonous verb errors. The error counts were translated into accuracy scores by considering them, in the case of syntactic errors, relative to the number of finite verbs produced; in the case of prepositions, relative to the number of obligatory contexts for prepositions; and in the case of verb errors, relative to the number of verb forms produced. Before moving on to a description of the tasks and scoring procedures used in measuring the discourse and sociolinguistic traits, it is useful to examine the results obtained by the grade 6 immersion students who took the grammar tests relative to native speakers of French also in grade 6.

The results reported in this paper are based on a sub-sample of sixty-nine French immersion students who were administered the entire battery of oral production, multiple choice and written production tests. These immersion students have been in a programme in which they were taught entirely in French in kindergarten and grade 1, about 80% in French in grades 2 to 4, about 60% in French in grade 5, and about 50% in French in grade 6 — the year they were tested. The comparison group of native French speakers consists of ten grade 6 students who likewise were administered the entire test battery. The native speakers of French were in a unilingual French school in Montreal. The results for the grammatical oral production, multiple choice and written production tasks are shown in Tables 1, 2 and 3 respectively. The essential point to note in these tables is that with the exception of correct use of homophonous verb forms, the native speakers score significantly higher ($p<.01$) than the immersion students, indicating clearly that, although the immersion students are doing quite well, they have not acquired native-like abilities in the grammatical domain.

The second trait measured, that of discourse competence, was defined as the ability to produce and recognize coherent and cohesive text. The discourse oral production task is designed to elicit narrative and argumentation. The students are shown a short nonverbal film, *The Mole and the Bulldozer,* chosen for its appropriateness to the age group of the students being tested, and for its provocative content which illustrates the conflict between modern technology and the preservation of nature. The day following the film's showing, students are taken individually from class and asked to tell the story of the film. A series of pictures of key events is placed in front of the child to minimize the burden on memory. Following the narration, the student is asked to role-play the mole and try to convince the bulldozers not to change the route of a road, using all the arguments he or she can think of.

TABLE 1

Grammatical Oral Production: Percentage Correct

	Immersion students		*Native speakers*		*Comparison*	
	Mean	*SD*	*Mean*	*SD*	*t*	*sig of t*
Syntax	81.3	13.1	96.5	6.8	3.60	.01
Prepositions	80.5	12.1	100.0	0.0	—	—
Verbs	57.0	18.1	96.4	5.1	6.79	.01
Total	73.2	8.6	96.9	4.0	8.56	.01

TABLE 2

Grammatical Multiple Choice: Percentage Correct

Immersion students		*Native speakers*		*Comparison*	
Mean	*SD*	*Mean*	*SD*	*t*	*sig of t*
60.7	4.41	81.3	4.40	6.20	.01

TABLE 3

Grammatical Written Production: Percentage Correct

	Immersion students		*Native speakers*		*Comparison*	
	Mean	*SD*	*Mean*	*SD*	*t*	*sig of t*
Syntax	75.5	12.1	93.6	6.9	4.60	.01
Prepositions	78.8	10.5	96.0	6.3	5.01	.01
Non-hom. verbs	85.5	7.2	95.9	4.6	4.49	.01
Hom. verbs	78.5	9.0	79.1	10.3	.20	ns
Total	70.9	8.7	85.0	8.5	4.82	.01

Scoring of the Story-retelling task was based on four categories:

1. setting the scene;
2. identification;
3. logical sequence of events;
4. time orientation.

Under the category of 'setting the scene,' the student's establishment of the idyllic habitat and lifestyle of the mole was assessed. This was important for the coherence of the story as it was this idyllic atmosphere that was at risk throughout. Under the category of 'identification,' the student was rated for the explicitness and clarity with which key characters, objects and locations were introduced into the narrative. Because the student had been given to understand that the interviewer had not seen the movie, it was incumbent on the student to name the characters, objects and locations. Under the category 'logical sequence of events,' a rating was given for the logical coherence with which the events of the story were narrated.

Thus it was important to explain how the mole knew the bulldozers were coming and would endanger his garden, and what the various steps were that the mole took to insure the safety of his property. And finally, under the category of 'time orientation,' a rating was given for the coherent use of verb tenses, temporal conjunctions, adverbials and other elements that clarified the temporal relationship between the events of the story. Each of these categories was rated on a scale of 1 (low) to 5 (high). The role-playing situation was also rated on a scale of 1 (low) to 5 (high) for the extent to which logical arguments were presented to support the mole's case that the road should not be straightened. And finally a global score of 1 (low) to 5 (high) was obtained representing the rates' subjective integration of scene setting, idenfitication, logic, time sequence and argument. The multiple choice test of discourse competence consists of twenty-nine items primarily measuring coherence. Each item is a short passage of two to five sentences. One sentence is omitted from the passage, and the task is to select the appropriate completion from a set of three alternatives.

The criterion for selection is primarily the logical coherence of the passage. Intersentential cohesive devices are explicitly incorporated in some items as a basis for choice. An example is given below:

Le premier voyage en ballon dirigible a eu lieu en France en 1783. ———————————Cependant ca a ete un grand evenement pour les francais.

(a) II n'a dure que 8 minutes.
(b) II avait ete bien planifie.
(c) II etait rempli d'air chaud.

The written discourse production tasks were the same ones used in the grammatical production tasks, two compositions involving narrative discourse and two letters involving suasion. Scoring for discourse involved six categories:

1. basic task fulfilment;
2. identification;
3. time orientation;
4. anaphora;
5. logical connection;
6. punctuation.

The assessment of 'basic task fulfilment' involved rating how well the written work fulfilled the basic semantic requirements of the discourse task. The qualify as narratives, for example, the compositions needed to include a series of events.

To qualify as suasion, the letters had to contain a request with at least one supporting argument. The category of 'identification' was similar to that for the oral production task in which an assessment was made of whether new characters, objects and locations were sufficiently identified, or whether too much prior knowledge on the part of the reader was assumed. The category of 'time orientation' was also similar to that use in the oral production task, assessing how adequately events or situations were located in time, and, where relevant, whether the temporal relationship between events or situations was clear. Under the category of 'anaphora,' the use of anaphoric reference to already identified characters, objects, or locations through the use of subject pronouns, possessive adjectives and articles was assessed. The category of 'logical connection' assessed the logical relationship between segments of the text: whether there were non-sequiturs, semantically obscure or fragmentary incidents, or logically missing steps in the argument or sequence of events. The final category, that of 'punctuation' was rated as an indication of the information structure of a text.

Ratings were based on the extent to which punctuation clarified the information structure of the text by indicating boundaries of information units. Each of these categories was rated on a five-point scale of 0 (low) to 2 (high). Following the detailed scoring, the raters who had scored the six discourse categories independently assigned a global discourse score by first sorting the written tasks into three categories of below average, average and above average, and then rating them as relatively high or low within each of these three categories. This resulted in a six-point scale. The criteria for assigning a global score were not closely specified: the scorers were simply asked to keep in mind the general criterion of coherent discourse. The discourse results are shown in Tables 4, 5 and 6 for oral production, multiple choice and written production tasks respectively.

On the separate aspects of discourse which were rated, examination of the comparisons between the immersion and native-speaker students reveals only two significant differences: in the case of oral production, native speakers are rated significantly higher than immersion students on time orientation (p<.01); and in the case of written production, native speakers are rated significantly lower than immersion students on punctuation (p<.01). The non-significant trend revealed by these comparisons, but indicated in the comparison of total discourse scores is that native speakers generally perform better than the immersion students on the oral story retelling task, but do not differ in their performance on the written production tasks. The only indication to the contrary is that the global

TABLE 4

Discourse Oral Production Ratings on a Scale from 1 (Low) to 5 (High)

	Immersion students		*Native speakers*		*Comparison*	
	Mean	*SD*	*Mean*	*SD*	*t*	*sig of t*
Scene	3.0	1.16	3.5	.85	1.43	ns
Identification	3.2	1.07	3.9	1.37	1.89	ns
Logic	2.9	1.29	2.9	1.37	.04	ns
Time	3.5	1.18	4.5	.71	2.54	.01
Argument	2.9	1.55	3.4	1.26	1.06	ns
Total	3.1	.79	3.6	.79	2.10	.05
Global	2.9	.88	3.6	1.04	2.16	.05

TABLE 5

Discourse Multiple Choice: Percentage Correct

Immersion students		*Native speakers*		*Comparison*	
Mean	*SD*	*Mean*	*SD*	*t*	*sig of t*
66.6	3.78	71.0	2.84	1.03	ns

score for the written production tasks shown in Table 6 reveals a significant difference (p<.05) between the mean scores obtained by the two groups in favour of the native speakers.

TABLE 6

Discourse Written Production: Ratings on a Scale from 0 (Low) to 2 (High)

	Immersion students		*Native speakers*		*Comparison*	
	Mean	*SD*	*Mean*	*SD*	*t*	*sig of t*
Basic	1.7	.28	1.8	.30	1.61	ns
Identification	1.3	.31	1.2	.25	- .58	ns
Time	1.5	.30	1.4	.38	- .47	ns
Anaphora	1.7	.24	1.6	.33	-.98	ns
Logic	1.5	.30	1.6	.35	1.34	ns
Punctuation	1.6	.41	1.2	.54	- 2.67	.01
Total	1.5	.19	1.5	.24	- .72	ns
Global	3.3	1.04	4.1	1.42	2.22	.05

There would seem to be two possible interpretations for the different results obtained by a comparison of the *total* written discourse scores from those obtained by a comparison of the *global* written discourse scores (Table 6). It may indicate that the raters were able to detect qualitative differences in the written discourse of native speakers and immersion students that were not captured in the detailed component scores, or it may be that the raters did not stay strictly within the bounds of discourse in making their global ratings. For example, if the raters inadvertently attended to grammatical aspects, which, as he been seen, are clearly better in the native-speaking sample, they may have rated the native speakers better for the wrong reason. At this point then, it can be seen that differences between the native and non-native groups depend on the trait being measured. For grammar, the difference is large regardless of method; for discourse, the difference is small regardless of method.

These results suggest that the grammatical trait is distinguishable from the discourse trait. The third trait measured, that of sociolinguistic competence, was defined as the ability to produce and recognize socially appropriate language within a given sociocultural context. The oral production sociolinguistic test consists of presenting a series of twelve situations using slides and audio accompaniment describing the situation. Each situation is a particular combination of one of three functions—request, suggestion or complaint; of one of two levels of formality — high or low; and of one of two settings — in school or out of school. The test begins with the tester explaining to the student being tested how different registers of speech may be used in different situations and illustrates this with an example. The student then watches a set of three slides and listens to the synchronized description.

With the showing of the last slide, the student responds in the most appropriate way as if addressing the person shown in the slide. For example, one set of slides shows two children in the school library who are the same age as the student being tested. The student hears a description, in French, that says 'You're in the library to study. But there are two persons at the next table who are speaking loudly, and are bothering you. You decide to ask them to make less noise. What would you say if the two persons were fiends of yours?' To change the level of formality, another set of slides shows two adults in the library, and the final question is 'What would you say if the two persons were adults that you don't know'? The objective of the scoring was to determine the extent to which students could vary their language use appropriately in response to the social demands of the different situations. In other words, the scores were t indicate the student's ability to use linguistic markers of formal register in formal situations and to refrain from using them in informal situations.

Thus, for each situation, a student's response was scored for the presence (= 1) or absence (= 0) of six markers of formal register. The six formal features were:

1. the use of an initial politeness marker such as *pardon* or *madame* in the utterance opening;
2. the use of *vous* as a form of address;
3. the use of question forms with *est-ce que* or inversion;
4. the use of the conditional verb form;
5. the inclusion of formal vocabulary and/or the use of additional explanatory information;
6. the use of concluding politeness markers such as *s'il vous plait.*

A student's score on a particular marker in a particular situation was taken as the difference between use of the marker in the formal variant of the situation and use in the informal variant. A good sociolinguistic score was thus a relatively high difference score, and a poor sociolinguistic score was a relatively low or negative difference score. The multiple choice test of sociolinguistic competence consists of twenty-eight items designed to test the ability of a student to recognize the appropriateness of an utterance with respect to its sociocultural context.

The items describe a specific sociocultural situation and the student is asked to select the best of three possible ways to express a given idea in that situation. The items are designed to include both written and spoken language use in varying degrees o formality, and include the identification of certain written styles such as those use in proverbs, in publications such as journals, encyclopaedias and magazines, and in public notices. Before starting the text, the distinction between oral and written language is drawn to the students' attention, and the students are told that the register of the responses, not their gramaticality, is the important consideration. Each item is scored according to the degree of appropriateness based on native-speaker responses, with values ranging from nought to three points.

Two examples are given below:

1. A l'ecole, dans la cour de recreation, dite par une eleve a son ami
   - (a) Pourrais-je te voir un instant?
   - (b) Est-ce que je pourrais te parler quelques minutes?
   - (c) Je peux te parler une minute?
2. Devant l'hotel de ville, ecrit sur un panneau public
   - (a) Priere de ne pas passer sur le gazon.
   - (b) Ne pas passer sur le gazon.
   - (c) Vous ne devez pas passer sur le gazon.

The sociolinguistic written production tasks focus on two extremes of directive. The students wrote two letters requesting a favour of a higher status, unfamiliar adult. In addition, the students wrote two notes in which they assumed the role of a familiar adult (mother, teacher) imposing authority by means of a brief informal note to get action from the student who is at fault in some way (has left room untidy, homework undone). As with the sociolinguistic oral production tasks, the scoring of the sociolinguistic written production tasks was designed to capture the student's ability to use formal sociolinguistic markers of politeness that were appropriate in the context of the letters, and to abstain from using such markers in the context of the notes.

Thus each letter and note were scored for the presence or absence of several formal markers:

1. the use of conditional verb forms;
2. the use of modal verbs, and/or *est-ce que,* inverted and indirect question forms, and/or the use of idiomatic polite expressions (e.g. *ayez l'obligeance de*);
3. the use of *vous* as a form of address;
4. the use of formal closings (e.g. *merci a l'avance, merci de votre collaboration*).

As with the sociolinguistic oral task, a difference score was calculated between the use of each marker in the formal contexts and its use in the informal contexts.

The sociolinguistic scores are shown in Tables 7, 8 and 9 for the oral production, multiple choice and written production tasks respectively. The results suggest that overall, native speakers perform significantly better on the sociolinguistic tasks than the immersion students. Excluding for the moment the use of *vous* as a polite form of address, the only discernibly pattern in the results is that in those categories of sociolinguistic performance where formulaic politeness terms are possible, immersion students tend to perform as well as native speakers, whereas in those categories where grammatical knowledge inevitably plays a role in the production of the appropriate form, immersion students' performance is inferior to that of native speakers.

This is especially obvious in the use of the conditional where immersion students perform relatively poorly on both written and oral tasks. This result is not particularly surprising in light of the grammatical results reviewed earlier. As Tables 1 and 3 immersion students are relatively weak in verb morphology. Here, then, appears to be a good example of the dependence of some aspects of sociolinguistic performance on grammatical knowledge.

TABLE 7

Sociolinguistic Oral Production : Difference Scores, Formal-Informal Use

	Immersion students		*Native speakers*		*Comparison*	
	Mean	*SD*	*Mean*	*SD*	*t*	*sig of t*
Introduction	.522	.263	.400	.263	-1.37	ns
Vous	.300	.220	.800	.132	6.97	.01
Question	.117	.180	.417	.180	4.96	.01
Conditional	.042	.150	.267	.210	4.22	.01
Other	.102	.167	.517	.183	7.25	.01
Finale	.095	.203	.200	.258	1.49	ns
Total	1.170	.530	2.600	.570	7.94	0.1

TABLE 8

Sociolinguistic Multiple Choice: Percentage Correct

Immersion students		*Native speakers*		*Comparison*	
Mean	*SD*	*Mean*	*SD*	*t*	*sig of t*
35.29	6.13	40.50	10.10	2.29	.05

TABLE 9

Sociolinguistic Written Production: Difference Scores, Formal-Informal Use

	Immersion students		*Native speakers*		*Comparison*	
	Mean	*SD*	*Mean*	*SD*	*t*	*sig of t*
Conditional	.195	.335	.700	.350	4.43	.01
MQP	.645	.365	.750	.355	.85	ns
Vous	.230	.350	1.000	.000	—	—
Closing	.405	.455	.650	.410	1.60	ns
Total	1.480	.840	3.100	.667	5.83	.01

The underuse of *vous* as a polite marker in formal contexts by immersion students as indicated in both Tables 7 and 9 can be linked directly to the input the students have received. Teachers address the students as *tu,* and students address each other as *tu.* The use of *vous* in the classroom setting is likely to be reserved for addressing groups of students, thus signalling its use as a plural form, or as a means of signalling annoyance on the part of the teacher.

There are thus few opportunities in the classroom for the students to observe the use of *vous* as a politeness marker used in differential status situations. The picture which emerges from these results, then, is one of a group of language learners who, although they have in some respects reached a high level of target language proficiency, are still appreciably different in their use of some aspects of the language from native speakers. This appears to be particularly evident in those aspects of communicative performance which demand the use of grammatical knowledge. These results are consistent with those we have found with grade 9 immersion students using a completely different set of tests (Lapkin, Swain and Cummins 1983).

Krashen (1981) has argued that learners 'acquire structure by understanding messages and not focusing on the form of input, by "going for meaning"' (p. 54). According to Krashen, this comprehensible input 'delivered in a low (affective) filter situation is the only "causative variable" in second language acquisition' (p. 57). Comprehensible input I take to mean language directed to the learner that contains some new element in it but that is nevertheless understood by the learner because of linguistic, paralinguistic or situational cues, or word knowledge back-up. It is different in nature, I think, from what Schachter (1984) has referred to as negative input includes, for example, explicit corrections, confirmation checks and clarification checks.

There is no reason to assume that negative input necessarily includes some new linguistic element in it for the learner. it may, for example, consist of a simple 'What?' in response to a learner utterance. As such it is basically information given to learners telling them to revise their output in some way because their current message has not been understood. The hypothesis that comprehensible input is the *only* causal variable in second language acquisition seems to me to be called into question by the immersion data just presented in that immersion students do receive considerable comprehensible input. Indeed, the immersion students in the study reported on here have been receiving comprehensible input in the target language for almost seven years.

One might question, then, whether the immersion students have in fact, been receiving comprehensible target language input. The evidence that they have, however, seems compelling. The evidence comes from their performance on tests of subject-matter achievement. For years now, in a number of French immersion programmes across Canada, immersion students have been tested for achievement in such subjects as mathematics, science, history and geography, for which the language of instruction has been French, and their performance has been compared to that of students enrolled in the regular English programme who are taught the same subject-matter content in their first language. In virtually all the comparisons the French immersion students have obtained achievement scores equivalent to those obtained by students in the regular English programme (Swain and Lapkin 1982).

Furthermore, on tests of listening comprehension in French, the immersion students perform as well as native speakers of French by grade 6. This strongly suggests that the immersion students understood what they were being taught, that they focused on meaning. Yet, as we have seen, after seven years of this comprehensible input, the target system has not been fully acquired. This is not to say that the immersion students' input is not limited in some ways. We have already seen that there are few opportunities in the classroom for the students to observe the use of *vous* as a politeness marker in differential status situations. I suspect also that the content of every-day teaching provides little opportunity for the use of some grammatically realized functions of language.

The use of the conditional may be a case in point. But until data are collected pertaining to the language actually used by immersion teachers, nothing further can be said on this point. It is our intention to collect such immersion teacher talk data in the near future. Another way in which the immersion students' input may be limited they do. But as is pointed out below, in the later grades of school, students are likely to hear more teacher talk than peer talk. And our own informal observations indicate that most peer-peer interaction that is not teacher directed is likely to occur in English rather than in French at this grade level. Given these possible limitations in input, the fact still remains that these immersion students have received comprehensible input in the target language for seven years.

Perhaps what this implies is that the notion of comprehensible input needs refinement. Long (1983), Varonis and Gass (1985), and others have suggested that it is not input *per se* that is important to second language acquisition, but input that occurs in interaction where meaning is negotiated. Under these conditions, linguistic input is simplified and the contributions made by the learner are paraphrased and expanded, thereby making the input more comprehensible. Given then, that comprehensible input is the causal variable in second language acquisition (Krashen 1981), the assumption is that second language acquisition results from these specific interactional, meaning-negotiated conversational turns. If this is the case, then, we may have part of the explanation for the immersion students' less than native-like linguistic performance.

In the context of an immersion class, especially in the later grade levels, and like in any first language classroom where teachers perceive their primary role as one of imparting subject-matter knowledge, the teachers talk and the students listen. As Long (1983) has indicated in the context of language classes, there are relatively few exchanges in classroom discourse motivated by a two-way exchange of information where both participants — teacher and student — enter the exchanges as conversational equals.

This is equally true of content classes, and immersion classrooms are no exception. Immersion students, then, have — relative to 'street learners' of the target language — little opportunity to engage in two-way, negotiated meaning exchanges in the classroom. Under these circumstances, the interaction input hypothesis would predict that second language acquisition would be limited. This prediction is consistent with the immersion students' performance if it is confined to grammatical acquisition. Confining this prediction to grammatical acquisition is compatible with what appears to be an assumption underlying the input interaction hypothesis — that second language acquisition is equivalent to grammatical acquisition. is equivalent to grammatical acquisition.

As has been indicated by the theoretical framework of linguistic proficiency used in this study, however, we consider second language acquisition to be more than grammatical acquisition, and to include at least the acquisition of discourse and sociolinguistic competence as well, in both oral and written modes. From this perspective, the relative paucity of two-way, meaning negotiated exchanges does not appear to have impeded the acquisition of discourse competence. Indeed, it seems likely that the diet of comprehensible, non-interactive, extended discourse received by the immersion students may account — at least in part — for their strong performance in this domain relative to native speakers. In short, what the immersion data suggest is that comprehensible input will contribute differentially to second language acquisition depending on the nature of that input, and the aspect of second language acquisition one is concerned with.

As is already suggested, the interaction input hypothesis is consistent with the prediction that immersion students will be somewhat limited in their grammatical development relative to native speakers because of their relatively limited opportunity to engage in such interaction. Although this provides a theoretically motivated and intuitively appealing explanation, I have several doubts about its adequacy. The doubts relate to two inter-related assumptions:

1. the assumption that it is the exchanges, themselves, in which meaning is negotiated that it is the exchanges, themselves, in which meaning is negotiated that are facilitative to grammatical acquisition as a result of comprehensible input;
2. the assumption that the key facilitator is input, rather than output.

The first assumption, that the exchanges themselves are facilitative to grammatical acquisition, rests on the possibility that a learner can pay attention to meaning and form simultaneously. However, this seems unlikely. It seems much more likely that it is only when the substance of the message is understood that the learner can pay attention to the means of expression — the form of the message being conveyed.

As Cross (1978), examining the role of input in first language acquisition, stated: By matching the child's semantic intentions and ongoing cognitions, (the mother's) speech may free the child to concentrate on the formal aspects of her expressions and thus acquire syntax efficiently.

In other words, it would seem that negotiating measuring—coming to a communicative consensus — is a necessary first step to grammatical acquisition. It paves the way for future exchanges, where, because the message is understood, the learner is free to pay attention to form. Thus comprehensible input is crucial to grammatical acquisition, *not* because the focus is on meaning, *nor* because a two-way exchange is occurring, but because by being understood—by its match with the learner's ongoing intentions and cognitions — it permits the learner to focus on form. But this would appear to be the sort of comprehensible input that immersion students do, in large part, receive. What, then, is missing? I would like to suggest that what is missing is output. Krashen (1981) suggests that the only role of output is that of generating comprehensible input. But I think there are roles for output in second language acquisition that are independent of comprehensible input. A grade 9 immersion student told me about what happens when he uses French. He said, 'I understand everything anyone says to me, and I can hear in my head how I should sound when I talk, but it never comes out that way.' (Immersion student, personal communication, Nov. 1980). In other words, one function of output is that it provides the opportunity for meaningful use of one's linguistic resources.

Smith (1978b, 1982) has argued that one learns to read by reading, and to write by writing. Similarly, it can be argued that one learns to speak by speaking. And one-to-one conversational exchanges provide an excellent opportunity for this to occur. Even better, though, are those interactions where there has been a communicative breakdown — where the learner has received some negative input — and the learner is pushed to use alternate means to get across his or her message. In order for native-speaker competence to be achieved, however, the meaning of 'negotiating meaning' needs to be extended beyond th usual sense of simply 'getting one's message across.' Simply getting one's message across can and does occur with grammatically deviant forms and socio-linguistically inappropriate language.

Negotiating meaning needs to incorporate the notion of being pushed towards the delivery of a message that is not only conveyed, but that is conveyed precisely, coherently and appropriate language. Negotiating meaning needs to incorporate the notion of being pushed towards the delivery of a message that is not only conveyed, but that is conveyed precisely, coherently and appropriately. Being 'pushed' in output, it seems to me, it is concept parallel to that of the *i* + *l* of comprehensible input. Indeed, one might call this the 'comprehensible output' hypothesis.

There are at least two additional roles in second language acquisition that might be attributed to output other than that of 'contextualized' and 'pushed' language use. One, as Schachter (1984) has suggested, is the opportunity it provides to test out hypotheses — to try out means of expression and see if they work. A second function is that using the language, as opposed to simply comprehending the language, may force the learner to move from semantic processing to syntactic processing. As Krashen (1982) has suggested: in many cases, we do not utilize syntax in understanding — we often get the message with a combination of vocabulary, or lexical information plus extra-linguistic information.

As such it is possible to comprehend input — to get the message—without a syntactic analysis of that input.[3] This could explain the phenomenon of individuals who can understand a language and yet can only produce limited utterances in it. They have just never got round to a syntactic analysis of the language because there has been no demand on them to produce the language. The claim, then, is that producing the target language may be the trigger that forces the learner to pay attention to the means of expression needed in order to successfully convey his or her own intended meaning. The argument, then, is